Wicked Tales
FROM THE
HIGHLANDS

Wicked Tales

FROM THE

HIGHLANDS

John P. King

THE
History
PRESS

Published by The History Press
Charleston, SC 29403
www.historypress.net

First published 2011

Manufactured in the United States

ISBN 978.1.60949.442.1

King, John P.
Wicked tales from the Highlands / John P. King.
p. cm.
ISBN 978-1-60949-442-1
1. Highlands (N.J.)--History--Anecdotes. 2. Atlantic Highlands (N.J.)--History--
Anecdotes. 3. Crime--New Jersey--Highlands--History--Anecdotes. 4. Corruption--z
New Jersey--Highlands--History--Anecdotes. 5. Criminals--z New Jersey--Highlands--
Biography--Anecdotes. 6. Crime--New Jersey--Atlantic Highlands--History--Anecdotes.
7. Corruption--z New Jersey--Atlantic Highlands--History--Anecdotes. 8. Criminals--z
New Jersey--Atlantic Highlands--Biography--Anecdotes. 9. Highlands (N.J.)--Biography--
Anecdotes. 10. Atlantic Highlands (N.J.)--Biography--Anecdotes. I. Title.
F144.H52K57 2011
974.9'46--dc23
2011039234

Contents

CONTENTS

Introduction

Let there be no doubt about it. The communities located in "the Highlands" are and have always been safe places to live and raise a family, both in the hills and in the low-lying areas touched by the waters of the Shrewsbury River and Sandy Hook Bay. However, like places everywhere, the good people of both Highlands and Atlantic Highlands have at times experienced their unwanted share of atrocious happenings. The stories of the events and actions described in this book are not for the purpose of denigrating the people or character of either town, but simply for the reader's historical education and amusement. Without a doubt, true crime stories in magazines, books, film and especially on television are very entertaining.

It is important to remember that "wicked" applies only to the actions and stories of these actions in this book; at no time should it be taken as a categorization of the towns or their people. It is thus used in a playful way.

The *Red Bank Register* (the primary source for these narratives), the *Courier of Middletown* and the *Asbury Park Press* contain just as many examples of benevolent and even, at times, heroic behavior on the part of the towns' people, especially in times of crisis. Unfortunately, however, those stories are yet to be written, published and enjoyed by readers. It is almost always the tragic accident, misfortune or violent crime that finds an audience.

As a counterbalance to this book, and for background information, the reader is urged to pick up and read the histories of the towns: *Highlands, N.J.* by John P. King (Making of America series, Arcadia Publishing, 2001) and *Atlantic Highlands, from Lenape Camps to Bayside Town* by Paul D. Boyd (Making

Replica of the *Half Moon*, ship of Henry Hudson, whose first mate Robert Juet in September 1609 described the Highlands as "a pleasant land to see," and so it has remained throughout history, bringing people to its many attractions.

of America series, Arcadia Publishing, 2004). There the reader can discover and appreciate the history of good people across time.

The term "the Highlands," as used throughout this book, should be understood to apply to the two boroughs of Atlantic Highlands and Highlands, lying geographically and culturally adjacent to each other, as well as to the land and waters of Sandy Hook, which have been closely related to the towns throughout history.

Part I

Crime in the Earliest Days

FIRST EUROPEAN MURDERED IN THE NEW WORLD

This crime was not only the first murder at Sandy Hook, just off the Highlands, it was also the first murder committed in North America, at least of a white European. The details come from *Juet's Journal*, written by Robert Juet, who sailed on the *Half Moon* with Henry Hudson in search of the Northwest Passage to the wealth of the East. Initially, relations between the Dutch explorers and the local Indians were civil. Hudson sent a boat crew into a Lenape village or camp in the Highlands hills and later welcomed some Indians aboard for more trade.

The next day, September 6, 1609, Hudson began exploring the area west of Sandy Hook up to the Raritan River, Newark Bay, the Kill Van Kull and the Narrows. Then something went terribly wrong late that afternoon: "Our Master sent John Coleman with four men in our boat over to the North-side…The men were set upon by two canoes, the one having twelve, the other fourteen men. The night came on and it began to rain so that their lamp went out. And they also had one man slain in the fight, which was an Englishman, named John Coleman, with an arrow shot into his throat, and two men hurt."

With only two men rowing, they got back to the *Half Moon* at about ten o'clock the next morning, bringing the dead man back for proper burial. John Coleman was buried on land, likely on Sandy Hook rather than on the

Above: Lenape Indians watch from the Highlands in awe, wonder and fear as the *Half Moon* arrives in Sandy Hook Bay.

Below: Stone arrowhead of the type that found its target in the neck of John Coleman of Henry Hudson's crew. *From the Paul Boyd Lenape Room of the Atlantic Highlands Historical Museum.*

bay shore mainland, where the burial party would have risked encountering more Lenape. Hudson named the spot "Coleman's Point."

The next day, the Lenape again came on board to trade, not revealing any hostility or cause for suspicion toward Hudson's men. However, Hudson expected a full-scale attack, distrusting the Lenape's friendliness. They raised the wooden sides on their boat as a protection from arrows and kept a careful watch all night long. At this point of deteriorated relations with the Lenape, Hudson left the Sandy Hook area to begin exploration of the river that would bear his name.

Indians Attack Again: Man Killed, Wife Left for Dead but Lived to Tell Her Story

A man named Van Princes and his new wife, Penelope, aged eighteen, sailed from their native Amsterdam to New Amsterdam (New York City) in 1640. Their marriage, though blessed by clergy, was ill-fated. First their ship was wrecked on Sandy Hook. Still worse was yet to come, though. The passengers and crew, however, all got ashore with their lives and some possessions, although Penelope's husband was badly hurt in the ordeal. On account of the hostile Indians known to be in the vicinity, the group did not feel safe remaining with the sick man. His wife refused to leave. They left Van Princes and Penelope as comfortable as they could and started overland to Staten Island and New Amsterdam, promising to send help to the couple as soon as possible. Their faith assured them that their prayers for the couple's and their own safety would be heard, although they knew well that the Indians had been on a rampage for some time throughout the area.

Penelope and her husband had not been in the woods very long before Indians found and attacked them, leaving Van Princes dead. However, Penelope was not killed, although she was knocked unconscious and horribly cut and mangled by the clubs and axes. Her left shoulder was so badly hacked that she would never use that arm like the other again. There was a long slash across her abdomen, causing her bowels to protrude. After the Indians had gone, Penelope held her intestines in place with her hand and managed to crawl for shelter into a hollow log, where she survived for a week.

Seeing a deer pass with arrows sticking in it, Penelope knew that Indians would soon follow. Two came along, one a young man and the other much

Penelope Stout was no doubt an attractive and accomplished woman, despite her horrific physical injuries at the hands of the Lenape.

older. She was glad to see the Indians, both hoping and fearing that they would put an end to her misery. The young Indian was about to club her on the head when the older man stopped him and threw Penelope over his shoulder, carrying her to his village, where he tended her wounds. She lived with the Indians for some time until the old Indian took her to the Dutch in New Amsterdam, perhaps to exchange her for a reward. Her condition improved.

In 1644, Penelope married Richard Stout in New Amsterdam. They moved to Graves End, Long Island, a year later, where Stout was a prominent landowner. Once the Dutch were forced from the New York area by the English, Richard and Penelope Stout moved to Monmouth County. Here in the Middletown and Holmdel area, Penelope lived until 1732, when she died at age 110, the progenitor of more than five hundred descendants.

Source: Stockton, Frank R. *Stories of New Jersey.* New York: American Book Company,1896.

Part II

When Murder Was Rare in the Early Highlands

The Butchery of Peter Finley

Charles Lord, the hotel's bartender, raced up the front steps and charged into James Jenkinson's office behind the house's front desk, out of breath and heaving.

"Calm yourself, man, will you. Let's not be disturbin' our lovely payin' guests, fine ladies and gentlemen, they are. Here now have a touch of this," Jenkinson offered. He motioned to the bottle of Irish whiskey he always kept at the right front corner of his huge desk.

"But Mr. Jenk…'s been a terr'ble thing. It's F…Finley," Lord gasped.

"Now be takin' it easy, Charlie. Finley? What about Finley. Still here is he? Just tell him for me to be off."

"Finley's been killed. Dead, I think," replied Lord.

Jenkinson's mind went spinning out of control. "Jesus, Mary and St. Joseph! No, it can't be. Not again. Not the Fourth of July holiday week! We're packed with people to the rafters, and some're beggin' to pay to sleep on the porches. Mother of God! At 71, I'm gettin' too old for this murder business. I think it'll kill me as well. My chest. What a pain. 'Twill pass, God have mercy." He poured an inch of whiskey into a glass for Lord and then two inches into another for himself. "Drink, man; we'll be needin' it. Now take and show me quick. God help us all. And be keepin' your voice low."

Jenkinson's Hotel had been a Highlands landmark destination for New York City people from 1868 to July 14, 1879, when the owner, James Jenkinson, died in the house—not murdered, but from a heart attack. Afterward, it was called the East View House.

On Wednesday, July 3, 1878, at the Highlands of Navesink, Peter Finley of Long Branch was killed by George Franklin, employed as a carver at Jenkinson's Hotel, who stabbed him with a large knife three times.

Old man Jenkinson had to agree with his son, James. Business had not only *not* fallen off but had actually increased. People from the other hotels in town—Thompson's, Swift's and Schenck's—came out of curiosity. Lots and lots of other people coming down from New York on the steamboat and New Jersey Southern Railroad got off at Highland station in Sea Bright and walked across the bridge just to see where the knifing had taken place, where the victim died. They (the gentlemen anyway) came in and had a drink at the bar, served by Charlie Lord, the eyewitness barkeeper. The ladies were served in a rear saloon. They had all read about the horrible murder in the local papers and in *all* of the city papers. The *Sun*, the *Herald*, the *Tribune* and the *Times* had all sent their reporters down not only for the news but also to stay the night, take meals and drinks. But how the devil could they get the facts so wrong? The page in the *Times* with the story wasn't worth wrapping dead fish in. James reminded his father that, as bad as it was, it was fine for business. He had cut it out and displayed it side by side with the local story:

When Murder Was Rare in the Early Highlands

New York Times
July 4, 1878

A BRUTAL MURDER IN NEW JERSEY
A Carver Stabs a Painter at Jenkinson's Highlands Hotel

LONG BRANCH, *July 3*—A cold-blooded murder was committed this evening at Jenkinson's hotel, at the Highlands of Navesink, eight miles from Long Branch. The name of the murdered man is Peter Finley, a sign painter formerly of New York, but lately a resident of Long Branch. The Police report the murderer to be James Franklin, a carver at Jenkinson's hotel. From what could be learned by THE TIMES reporter, it appears that James Jenkinson Jr., the son of the proprietor of the Highlands hotel, came to Long Branch last night and persuaded Finley, who was working here, to leave his job and go and do some painting at the Highlands. Finley went to work decorating the dining room between meal hours. In the afternoon, it is said that Finley and Franklin had some words, and that Franklin who is a troublesome person, tried to enrage Finley but failed. Franklin had begun preparing his meats for supper, and was cutting them on a table, when some of the paint from Finley's brush spattered the meats. This aroused Franklin's ire and he poured abuse upon Finley, and Finley retaliated by mimicking Franklin's remarks in broad Irish. This so incensed Franklin that he jumped toward Finley and brandishing a large carving knife in his hand, threatened to "cut him" if he did not desist. In reply, Finley dipped his brush in his paint pot and again bespattered the meats on the carving table. This so enraged Franklin that he caught Finley around the neck, and exclaiming, "Now I'll fix you," he plunged the carving knife three times into the painter's side. No one but Finley and Franklin were in the dining room at the time of the affray, but Finley's cries reached the ears of William Jenkinson, the clerk of the hotel, who, on rushing into the dining room, found Franklin leaning over his prostrate victim. Finley lived but a few moments after Mr. Jenkinson entered the room. He could only exclaim, "That man did it," and then expired. The murderer, who looked dazed, and seemed to scarcely comprehend the deed he had committed, was immediately put under arrest. Finley was about thirty years of age and was considered a hard working and steady young man. He lived with his married sister, a Mrs. Riddy, in Clark Street, Long Branch. The coroner at the Highlands telegraphed to the sister the intelligence of the tragic death of her brother, but she was absent when the dispatch arrived, and it was *opened by his brother, who had come down tonight to visit him. The brother was almost crazed at the startling intelligence. He left for the Highlands at a late hour to-night to take charge of his brother's body.*

The new Red Bank paper, called the *Red Bank Register* (its first edition coming out on June 27), practically doubled its circulation because of the murder. Tall stacks of the paper were dropped off by the steamboat. Old man Jenkinson was reading the story now. He smiled when he read "Jenkinson's Hotel" in the first sentence. Publicity was good, especially free publicity. Classified advertising in the *Times* cost so dear.

Red Bank Register
July 11, 1878

A MURDER AT THE HIGHLANDS
An Old Man Named Franklin Kills a Young Man Named Finley. The Murderer Arrested and Lodged in the County Jail.

About 5 o'clock on Wednesday afternoon of last week a murder was committed at the Highlands by George Franklin, a carver in Jenkinson's Hotel.

Finley, the murdered man, was a painter by trade and was employed by Mr. Jenkinson to paint signs for the bathing houses. Instead of returning to his home at Long Branch after finishing and being paid for the work, he remained about the Highlands and indulged in drinking. He stopped at Jenkinson's and at breakfast on the morning of the fatal day, a dispute arose between him and Franklin in regard to the food, and abusive language was used by both parties. Finley remained about the Highlands throughout the morning and when he went for his dinner the quarrel was renewed. He asked Franklin to give him something to eat and Franklin responded by calling Finley a "beggar of cold victuals" and a tramp. Finley then went to the upper bar room of the hotel and complained to the bar attendant of the harsh treatment he had received from Franklin. While talking to the bar tender, Franklin came in, and when Finley went up to him and said, "Old man, you ought to apologize to me," Franklin again began to abuse Finley, when the latter went out and walked toward the dining room, Franklin following him. What transpired in the dining room is not known, but the next time that the pair was seen was at 5 o'clock when they stood outside of the kitchen, apparently in hot dispute about something. Finley then went to the lower bar room, and, according to the testimony of Charles Lord, the bar tender, was there half an hour, when

Franklin, in shirt sleeves, came in and began to abuse Finley again. Finley had just taken several drinks and retaliated by threatening to kick Franklin out of the place. The bar keeper interfered and told Finley he had better go out and leave the old man alone. Finley went out as ordered, when Franklin followed him to the road, and putting his hand into the waist band of his trousers, he told Finley that if he did not retract something which he had said, that he would cut him. The reply that Finley made was to slap Franklin's face and say: "Old man, those gray hairs of yours save you from a licking." As the words came from Finley's mouth, Franklin pulled out a large carving knife and plunged it three times at Finley, cutting him in the right breast, in the left breast and in the arm. Finley staggered to the bar room and exclaimed: "Old man, my God, why did you cut me with a saw?" Then he fell on the bar room floor. Dr. Patterson of Navesink, was summoned and when he arrived Finley was dead.

Justice William C. Irwin of Red Bank summoned a jury and held an inquest on the body where it lay in the bar room. Several witnesses were called and testified as follows:

ALBERT HAVENS, sworn. I reside in Middletown township. Entered the bar room of the hotel and saw the deceased and the prisoner talking together. I then went away and when I returned I saw the prisoner put a knife under his apron. The deceased had blood dripping from his sleeve; as I was going out I heard him fall on the floor.

JOSEPH LAYTON, sworn. I saw the deceased and the prisoner talking together; could not tell what they were saying; saw the prisoner strike at the deceased four times; saw the blood flowing from the sleeve of the deceased.

JOHN REID, sworn. I saw the prisoner draw a knife from under his apron and strike at the deceased three times; the deceased struck the prisoner in the face three or four times.

DR. PATTERSON of Navesink, sworn. I made a post-mortem examination. There are two wounds upon the chest, one extending downward toward the medium line, which is necessarily a mortal wound; one beneath the axilla, and one in the middle of the left forearm; the first wound caused death by internal hemorrhage.

After an hour's deliberation the jury returned their verdict. Upon the suggestion of some gentleman present, who saw the irregularity of the verdict, it was rewritten in proper form. Finley's body was sent to his sister's home at Long Branch.

At the arrival of the steamboat Helen *the murderer was arrested by Officer Vanderhoof and taken to Red Bank where he was arraigned before*

Justice Child. The prisoner was not represented by counsel and refused to say anything about the tragedy. Upon complaint of Charles Lord, the bar tender at Jenkinson's Hotel, Franklin was committed to the lock up over night. On Thursday morning he was conveyed to the county jail, at Freehold, by Officer Patterson.

The knife with which the murder was committed was found in the staircase. Finley's bloody clothing had been buried, but at the request of Prosecutor Lanning, it was unearthed and will be used in evidence at the trial.

The murdered man was named Peter Finley, was 32-years-old, and resided with his sister at Long Branch. He was quite well educated and is said to have been of a fine disposition, although at times addicted to drink.

Franklin claims to be an American by birth; his permanent home being in New York. For the past few years he had been employed during the summer at Jenkinson's Hotel.

Prosecutor John E. Lanning, of Long Branch, is working up the case.

The original faulty coroner's verdict read: "We, the jury, find that Peter Finley, the deceased, came to his death by cuts inflicted upon him by George Franklin, and that we, the jury, find him guilty of murder in the first degree." The revised coroner's verdict read as follows:

New Jersey: Monmouth County.
An inquisition indented and taken at the Highlands of Navesink in the county aforesaid on 3rd day of July 1878 before me William C. Irwin one of the Justices of the Peace, upon the view of the body of Peter Finley, then and there lying dead, upon the oaths of Jacob Swan foreman, Robert Bradley, Levi Maxson, John Emery, John Reardon, Job Lyman, Albert Havens, John Wilson, Joshua Johnson, Theodore Bonlisler, James Hartsgrove, Thomas King good and lawful men of the county aforesaid who being sworn and charged to inquire on the part of the State of New Jersey, when, where, how and after what manner the said Peter Finley came to his death, do say upon their oaths that the one George Franklin late of the township of Middletown in the county aforesaid, did on the 3rd day of July 1878, at the township of Middletown in the county aforesaid willfully and feloniously kill and murder the said Peter Finley by use of a knife which George Franklin then and there held in his hand.

When Murder Was Rare in the Early Highlands

Signed: Jacob Swan, Robert X Bradley {his mark}, Levi Maxson, John Emery, John Reardon, Job G. Liming, Albert Havens, John H. Wilson, Joshua X Johnson {his mark}, T. Bonlisler, James Hartsgrove, Thomas King.

Franklin knew that his own life would be at risk if found guilty in court in the fall. He needed the best legal defense possible, although he had no money to pay for it. Henry M. Nevius, of the famed Red Bank law firm of Applegate and Nevius, agreed to represent Franklin pro bono and set to work collecting material to be used in the case that he realized would be difficult, even for him. This action was typical of Nevius, a champion of American rights since the Civil War, when he lost his arm in battle.

It had been a good season in 1878, a very profitable summer for all of the hotels along the shore from the Highlands to Long Branch and well beyond. A prolonged period of warm, dry weather brought record numbers of hotel vacationers and day-stay excursionists. Jenkinson's Hotel was exceptionally busy. It seemed that everyone wanted to stand on the site where the murder took place. What began as tragic progressed to horrible, terrible and coldblooded, finally becoming gruesome and savage. By the middle of October, the crowds were mostly gone and Jenkinson and his staff were closing up for the year. They kept just a few rooms available, as well as scaled-down versions of the restaurant and the bar (the murder scene), just in case the weather was warm enough and the trial down in Freehold brought any visitors to the Highlands. The following article introduces the case:

Red Bank Register
October 17, 1878

On Trial for His Life
George Franklin Arraigned for the Killing of Peter Finley—The Evidence in the Case—A Verdict of Murder in the Second Degree.

The trial of George Franklin for the murder of Peter Finley, a Long Branch sign painter, at the Highlands, on the 3rd of July last, was begun in Freehold on Monday last [October 14], in the Court of Oyer and Terminer, before a full bench with Judge E. W. Scudder presiding.

The accounts of this murder as reported in the news papers at the time and since have been so conflicting that a short resume of the facts gathered by a Register reporter will not be out of place.

THE TRUE AND ACCURATE ACCOUNT

Peter Finley had been employed by the Jenkinsons at the Highlands at various times during the last few years to do painting for them. When sober he was a good natured fellow and made friends with everybody, but when in liquor, which was often, he was quarrelsome.

George Franklin, a man nearly 70-years-old had long been employed by the Jenkinsons as a carver.

Franklin and Finley had frequently met at the hotel on the Highlands, but had failed to become friends, so that at the time of the killing there was an old feud between them.

On Wednesday the 3rd of July last, the men had become involved in a quarrel while Finley was in the kitchen at dinner. Finley was somewhat under the influence of liquor and very abusive in his language toward Franklin. After eating his dinner, Finley left the hotel but not without threatening Franklin. Toward the latter part of the afternoon Franklin went down the hill in front of the hotel for the purpose of seeing Mr. Lord who was the bar tender there.

At the entrance of the bar room he encountered Finley who accosted him in a threatening manner saying that his [Franklin's] gray hair was all that prevented him [Finley] from giving him a good thrashing. As Finley said this he knocked Franklin's hat off but was prevented from further violence by the interference of Mr. Lord. Franklin requested Finley to go away, as he did not wish to have anything to do with him. Mr. Lord, after separating the men, turned to go into the bar room and was just entering the door when a remark from Finley caused him to turn about and as he did so he saw Finley strike Franklin in the face with the flat of his hand two or three times and instantly Franklin drew a knife and plunged it three times into Finley. Franklin turned about and walked up the steps heading to the top of the hill, throwing away the knife as he went. Finley walked into the bar room, fell headlong upon the floor and in a few minutes was dead. An hour afterwards the steamer Helen arrived at the Highlands with Constable Vanderhoof on board, who arrested Franklin and took him to Red Bank. He was taken before Justice Child who committed him to jail. The next morning he was removed to the Freehold jail, not, however, before he had an interview with Mr. Henry M. Nevius, his counsel. Mr. Nevius, without fee or hope of reward, at the request of the prisoner, undertook his defense with all the ardor and industrious perseverance for which he is becoming noted.

For fully an hour before the time for the Court to open the people crowded into the court room until at half past ten the room was filled to overflowing, *with people standing in the aisles and doorways. At eleven o'clock by order of the presiding judge the prisoner was brought into the court accompanied by Sheriff Brown and several deputies. Franklin's appearance has changed for the better since the evening he appeared before Justice Child. At that time clad in a red shirt and smooth shaven face and evidently laboring under intense excitement, the impression made by the prisoner was not a very favorable one. On Monday morning as he came into court his appearance was eminently respectable. A full white beard covered his face, he wore a blue frock coat, and had all appearance of a man somewhat above the average. Taking his seat beside his counsel, inside the bar, the call for a jury began.*

The process of selecting a jury was finished in half an hour. The jury selected was as follows: Joseph Atkinson, G.H. Quackenbush, Emlin Satterwaith, Charles Perrine, Condit B. Smock, William W. Algor, John A. Baird, Robert C. Schenck, William Strickland, William Robbins, Hamilton Tabor and Alfred Cooper. None was a Highlands resident. The state's opening statement was as follows:

The Prosecutor Hon. John E. Lanning was assisted by Attorney General John P. Stockton in conducting the prosecution. Mr. Lanning opened the case for the State by reading the indictment to the jurors following it with a statement of the case: The prisoner and the deceased were employed at the hotel of Mr. Jenkinson. On the morning of the murder there had been words between the men. During the afternoon they met at the bar room under the hill. The prisoner refused an apology that was demanded of him by the deceased. An altercation took place and the prisoner drew from under his apron an old carving knife and stabbed the deceased three times, which caused his death.

Following are testimonies of witnesses:

CHARLES LORD was the first witness sworn for the State and testified as follows—I reside at the Highlands and had charge of the bar at Jenkinson's hotel; I last saw Finley on July 3rd at 4:30 o'clock. Finley was at that time in front of the bar; the prisoner came down the hill; I was inside the bar tending to my business; I heard Franklin and Finley talking outside; the prisoner was sitting in a chair when I went out; Finley had his hands on Franklin's shoulders demanding an apology for what he had said in the morning; Finley afterwards slapped the prisoner's face; I separated them and thinking the trouble ended I turned to go into the barroom; hearing words I turned and saw Franklin strike Finley twice with a knife; Finley came into the barroom and asked me to get him some water; as I turned to get a pail, Finley fell on the floor; I went up the hill and informed Mr. Jenkinson; I afterwards went for a doctor; at the time Franklin struck, Finley had his arm up; I saw two or three blows.

Cross-examined by Mr. Nevius.

{A photograph of the scene of the murder was here shown witness.} Franklin came down the hill at about 4 o'clock; he was there half an hour before I heard the disturbance; he was in the habit of coming down almost every afternoon; Franklin was sitting near the edge of the stoop when Finley put his hands on his shoulders; Finley said, "You have got to take that back." Franklin replied, "Go away and let me alone." I saw Franklin get up; I did not see Finley push him back into the chair; I heard Finley say, "You are not going away till you take that back." I saw Finley strike him before I interfered; I told Finley Franklin was an old man and I would not let him strike him; Franklin was behind me on the stoop; I then went to the bar; I heard a noise and turned and saw Franklin strike Finley; Franklin followed Finley one or two steps when he struck the last blow. {Counsel for the defense here showed the witness a map of the place where the altercation took place and the witness explained to the jury the situation of the men when Franklin struck, also the direction taken by Finley after he was struck.} Did not see what took place when my back was turned; Franklin did not follow Finley out to the main walk; Franklin did not pursue Finley; Finley said as he came into the barroom, "That is a nice thing to cut a man with an old saw;" Franklin had his apron on; he generally did when he came down.

GEORGE HARTSGROVE sworn. I reside at the Highlands; I was there on the 3rd of July last; I have seen Finley here; know Franklin by sight; they were on the stoop of the lower barroom on July 3rd; I heard Franklin say, "Damn you. If I must do it, I'll do it." I then saw him stab him with a butcher knife; I did not see him strike more than twice; Finley was trying to slap the old man when he stabbed him; I saw Finley take the old man's hat off and heard him say, "Nothing but your gray hair saves you from a licking and you must take it back." The last I saw of Franklin I saw him put his knife away and walk off.

Cross-examination. I saw Finley slap Franklin before the stabbing; Franklin was standing on the edge of the porch; after he was stabbed Finley *retreated toward the picket fence; Franklin did not come down off the porch after the stabbing.*

JOHN REED *sworn. Reside at the Highlands; on the 3rd of July last I was walking from Swift's to Jenkinson's as this matter occurred; I saw Finley strike Franklin in the face; Lord and Stillwell interfered and told Finley to go away and not hurt the old man; Lord turned to go into the barroom and the men advanced toward each other and Franklin said, "If I must use this I will"; then he drew his knife and stabbed Finley three times; I did not hear any threats by Finley; Finley lived about fifteen minutes; Franklin struck Finley with what I thought was an old butcher knife.*

Cross-examination. *I was by a little tree when the stabbing was done; I saw Finley's body after it was stripped; one wound was back of the arm pit; the wound on the right side was between the second and third ribs, two to two and a half inches from the nipple and a little below the nipple; the wound on the arm was a diagonal stab not a cut.*

WILLIAM P. SMITH *sworn. I live at Riceville; was employed at Jenkinson's on the 3rd of July last; I was not at the barroom when the difficulty occurred; Peter Vanderhoof came after Finley's clothes the day after; I had them buried;* {Here some clothes was shown and identified as the clothes of Peter Finley.}

DR. ROMEO F. SCHUBERT *sworn. Am a practicing physician and surgeon at Hoboken; July 3rd I was sitting on a stoop at Thompson's waiting for a boat; a man came along very much excited; he said he wanted a physician; a gentleman pointed me out and I accompanied him; I found a man lying on the floor of the barroom; I turned him over and he gave out one gasp and died; I found a wound in the chest about two or three inches from the right nipple; the wound was a mortal one; I inserted my fingers into the wound.*

DR. WILLIAM F. PATTERSON *sworn. I reside in Middletown; was called to the Highlands on July 3rd 1878; I was called to examine wounds on the body of a man who was killed there; there were three wounds—one under the left arm, one on the left arm, one beneath the right breast; the wound on the right breast was mortal; it was three inches deep; its direction backward;* {Knife shown witness.} *I should think the wounds were made with some such instrument; the wound in the left arm was between the bones; the arm must have been up when the wound under it was given.*

JOSEPH LAYTON *sworn. …after the stabbing Franklin turned and went up the steps; there are three pair of steps; Franklin went up the middle pair.*

ELIAS STILWELL sworn. *I was at the Highlands on the 3ʳᵈ of July last; Franklin and myself was sitting on the bar stoop talking…Franklin went toward the steps after the stabbing; I saw a knife lying under the willow tree the next morning;* {Knife shown witness.} *That looks like the knife.*

JEFFERSON COTTRELL sworn. *I live at the Highlands, was not there on the 3ʳᵈ of July; I found a knife after the 3ʳᵈ; I have seen that knife in Mr. Franklin's hands a good many times at the meat shop of Mr. Jenkinson; I found the knife in the willows; I keep my oars there; I have seen Mr. Franklin use the knife to take bones out with.*

Cross-examined. *I found the knife on the 5ᵗʰ; I had it in my possession six or seven days; nobody told me the knife was there; the willow tree is about ten yards from the steps; could not see the knife from the walk; in placing my oars along side the willow I saw the knife; I was at the Highlands when Mr. Throckmorton made the map; I do not remember showing anybody the place where the knife was found.*

GEORGE PARKER sworn. *On the 3ʳᵈ last I was at the Highlands. I was driving by and saw Mr. Franklin stab Finley.*

PETER VANDERHOOF sworn. *I am a constable. I know George Franklin. On July 3ʳᵈ last I was on the steamer* Helen. *We reached the Highlands at 5 o'clock. Mr. Jenkinson came on board and asked me to arrest a man. I went with him and arrested Franklin. He asked me what I was going to do with him. I told him I was going to take him to Red Bank. The Sunday after the 4ᵗʰ of July I got the knife* {shown knife} *from Jefferson Cottrell.*

The second day of the trial was mainly spent in the examination of witnesses for the prosecution, whose testimony tended to corroborate that of the prior witnesses. Here the state rested, and Mr. Nevius opened for the defense in a short address, going over the defense briefly:

During the testimony of the defense, the prisoner sat with a handkerchief, evidently weeping. His whole demeanor was that of an old man almost totally broken down in spirits.

James Jenkinson sworn. *Reside at the Highlands; knew Finley; he came to the Highlands on the 1ˢᵗ of July between 5 and 6 o'clock P.M. to paint signs for me; he did the painting on Tuesday the 2ⁿᵈ; I settled with him on Tuesday evening; he had no further business there after that; I saw him the next morning between 10 and 11 o'clock; He was on the beach about fifty or sixty feet from the New Jersey Southern Rail Road station; he was there before the train went; I asked him to go home on the 11:59 train; he said he had no money; I said I would give him money to go home; he said, "No, give me money to get a drink to brace myself up." I gave him a quarter; I next saw him coming from Maxson's; he went behind the station house while the train passed; he said he went there to avoid being seen by anyone from Long Branch; I saw him in our kitchen; Mr. Franklin was in front of him; Finley was eating; Finley said Franklin called him a "dead beat and a cold meat grubber." Finley then began quarrelling with Franklin. Franklin said nothing to Finley; that was the last I saw of him alive.*

Cross-examination. *Have lived at the Highlands for eleven years; I employed Finley; I paid him off at about 7 o'clock on the evening of the 2nd of July; Finley said Franklin called him a dead beat, a sucker, a cold meat grubber; I had the body of Finley washed and wrapped in one of our quilts; the body was removed to Long Branch the next morning on the first passenger train; Finley's clothes were in a pail; I told Albert Havens to bury them and let me know where so that I could get them if they were wanted.*

Cornelius Conover sworn. *Am ticket agent at the Highlands; was on 3rd of July last.* {Witness produced time table of N.J.S.R.R. of July last and gave time of train}.

Jacob Swan sworn. *Reside at the Highlands; am bridge tender there; on 3rd of July last saw Finley cross the bridge for the 2:31 train; when he came back the train had left; I asked him what he was crossing the bridge so much for; he said, "To save funeral expenses;" Mr. Johnson then came up and I introduced Finley to Johnson; they went off toward Schenck's place; afterwards I saw them going toward Jenkinson's.*

Tylee W. Throckmorton, sworn. *Live at Red Bank; made the map of the Jenkinson place.*

Following were defense character witnesses:

LYDIA WEBSTER, sworn. *Reside in New York; lived at Jenkinson's in July last; knew Franklin and Finley; remember their being in the kitchen on the 3rd; Franklin was carving; Finley asked for a piece of meat; Franklin paid no attention to him; after Finley went out Franklin said, "I have been a friend to that man and have kept him from starving."*

CHARLES JOHNSON, sworn. *Reside at Navesink; was at the Highlands on the 3rd of July last; fell in with a man [Finley] at he bridge on that day and went with him to Schenck's.*

JAMES JENKINSON, recalled. *Franklin has been in my employ seven or eight years as a carver and preparer of meat; I found him a sober, quiet, and industrious man; his reputation for peace was good as far as I know.*

MILES SMITH, sworn. Reside in New York; have known Franklin twenty years; has been in my employ at different times; he is a peaceable, quiet man so far as I know; never saw him drink anything.

O.O. BRANCH, sworn. Have kept a restaurant in New York a number of years; have known Franklin for twelve years; his character for peace and quietness was good.

A.F. FOWLER, sworn. Reside at Oceanic [Rumson]; have known Franklin since 1860 or 1861; worked for me in 1870; never saw him take more than one or two drinks.

Then the defendant Franklin took the stand:

In testifying in his own behalf he seemed to gain courage and told his story in a straightforward manner that convinced almost everyone of its truth.

GEORGE FRANKLIN, sworn. I was born in Sussex county, N.J. I am 69 years and 10 months old; during the last six or seven years I have worked in the summer time at Jenkinson's. I knew Peter Finley. First saw him there three years ago; our relations were friendly; next met him a year afterwards at the same place; it was at the lower bar; he was under the influence of liquor; he asked me if I did not know him; I said I did; I then went up to the house; he then came up there and said, "Franklin, for God's sake give me something to eat, for nobody around here will pay any attention to me." I sat him down at the table and went and got him some meat; I took it to him; and took some bread, butter, potatoes, etc. I also asked somebody to get him some more tea; I never saw him afterwards until he came to paint some signs on the 2nd of July last; he and Jenkinson were at that time arranging to paint the signs that day when I was in the kitchen cutting the food for the help, I stood with my back to the tables where the help were eating; I turned around and saw Finley turned half way round in his chair; I told him to go away, I can't be bothered when I am cutting meat; he said, "I want something nice." That is all I heard; he went away; I then told the people about his first visit the year before; I next saw him between 12 and 1 the next day; I was in the meat shop putting away some meat; Finley came; he said to me, "Franklin, I want an apology;" I said, "Go away and don't bother me." He said, "I want you to tell me what you said." I sent him away; I said he ought to be the last man to come here and pick a quarrel with me; I reminded him that I once fed him; he said if it were not for my gray hair, he would give me a thrashing; I said that if I were a young man I would clean out a whole lot such as you; he then went off; I was glad of it for I did not want to have trouble with him; I did not care what he said as long as he did not do anything; I went to the house and cut the dinner; then I went back to the meat house; {knife shown witness} that is my knife; I wanted that knife to cut the cold meats for supper; I took the knife and I started for the dining room, but went down the hill first to get a drink, putting the knife in my pocket; I spoke to Mr. Lord, then sat down beside Mr. Elias Stilwell; the next thing I heard was Finley in front of me; he said, "Franklin you must take that back." I told him to go away; he had his hand on my shoulder; I tried to get up and he pulled me back down in the chair; I then got up and he pulled my hat off; he then said, "I told Mr. Jenkinson what you said." He said you are a damned old fool; he then struck me a blow; Mr. Lord came out and put his hand on him and told him not to hit so old a man; Finley then put his hand around Lord and hit me in the face; Lord turned away and Finley sprung at me and caught me by the shoulder and pulled me toward him; I thought he would give me a sound beating so I pulled out this knife and pushed it at him thinking to cut his hands so that he would let me go; he then went into the bar and I up to the hill; I often carry a knife back and forth from the kitchen to the meat shop; I either dropped or threw the knife away as I went up the hill. Here the defense rested.

Following was the summation for the state:

Mr. Lanning opened for the State in summing up, saying: "There is no doubt, gentlemen of the jury, but that there has been a grave crime committed. The defense admits this. They admit the knife with which the crime was committed. I am surprised, gentlemen, that there have not been more mitigating circumstances shown by the defense. A killing done in the heat of passion may be murder in the second degree, but we assume the position that this was a case of murder in the first degree. There was an old feud between these men from which nothing can be inferred in this case except murder."

The counsel then went over the evidence claiming that it proved beyond any possible doubt that Franklin advanced upon the victim showing malice. The counsel called attention to the fact that the victim had no weapon, that Franklin was surrounded by friends able to protect him, who had protected him, and that it was the third stab that was the fatal one. These facts taken together with the fact that Franklin threatened to cut Finley's heart out, the counsel contended, proved malice beyond a doubt.

Following was the summation for the defense:

> *Mr. Nevius began summing, making in the course of a long and powerful argument, the following points: The course of the press, referring to the article in the New York* Herald *the day the Grand Jury met and to the article in the* New York Times *which was so harmfully inaccurate; the matter of premeditation, citing the differences between the Donnelly case and this one; that conviction of murder in the first degree was not consistent with the indictment; that even a verdict of manslaughter was inconsistent with the evidence; that an acquittal based on self-defense was required. At the conclusion, after two long hours, the Court adjourned till ten o'clock on Wednesday morning.*

On the third day, the following events transpired, as reported:

> *A Number of Ladies in Attendance*
> *The Attorney General began his argument at 10:20, speaking slowly and impressively, with a coolness and deliberation. He said that this case was in a nutshell: the malice of the prisoner, the gentleness of the murdered man, the evidence reviewed proved guilt, the prisoner admitted his crime. He spoke for one hour and forty minutes.*

> *Judge Scudder Charges the Jury*
> *The Judge went into the law of homicides and in a clear and impartial manner expounded the law of murder in the first and second degrees, and of manslaughter. He then went over the evidence in the case, applying the principles of law to the facts as sworn to. At the conclusion of the regular charge, by request of the prisoner's counsel, he made a special charge on points of law stated by counsel. Forty minutes were consumed in delivery of the charge. It was listened to with breathless silence by the crowd in the court room.*

> *Jury Deliberates*
> *At twenty minutes of one the jury retired. They remained out all night and on Thursday morning the jury delivered its verdict of "guilty of murder in the second degree."*

Justice was swift back in the nineteenth-century legal system, in which even a three-day trial was unusually long, and sentencing followed immediately upon the delivery of the jury's verdict, here on the fourth day.

When Murder Was Rare in the Early Highlands

Red Bank Register
October 21, 1878

FRANKLIN SENTENCED

George Franklin, the aged man, who was convicted of murder in the second degree for killing Peter Finley at the Highlands of Navesink, on July 3, was before Judge Scudder for sentence. The Judge said, after consultation with his colleagues, the Court entirely approved the finding of the jury. Although the New Jersey statute does not authorize imprisonment for life for this crime, they had determined to impose a sentence which, to a man in his seventieth year, would be equivalent to a life sentence, namely, ten years in the State prison.

Additional sources: *New York Times,* July 4 and October 6, 15–18, 22.

Part III

Wicked Days of Prohibition and Rumrunning

A WICKED AND DEADLY MIX: SOLDIERS, LOOSE WOMEN, WHISKEY AND HIGHLANDS

Strife between soldiers on Sandy Hook and the residents of Highlands can be traced as far back as the early days of the Civil War, when troops were posted there to protect the peninsula and New York from possible Confederate attack and capture. The men at both the Sandy Hook Proving Grounds and the newer Fort Hancock artillery post quickly formed an all too often troubled relationship with the men and women in the nearest town, Highlands. For as long as anyone could remember, a less than legal, and potentially dangerous, enterprise was carried on, under cover of darkness, by boats across the Shrewsbury River and Sandy Hook Bay separating the areas. Most of the time, this activity was mutually beneficial, and little notice was made of it. However, occasionally tempers fed by whiskey and beer heated and flared up into threats, physical violence and even murder.

Early on Friday, May 13, 1904, Charles Stratton was shot and killed by George H. Wasson, a soldier from Fort Hancock, in a hotel in Highlands. Wasson, whose home was in rural Virginia, had been stationed on guard duty at the north end of the wooden railroad trestle that spanned the low and often flooded area at the beginning of the sandy peninsula just beyond the Highland Beach resort area of William Sandlass. Later, a stone seawall would eliminate the need for the trestle, and a road would connect the military area with the strip of north Sea Bright. At this time, the railroad was the only land link, and it was a vital one, requiring armed guard protection.

This soldier left his post after dark at about eight o'clock on Thursday, May 12, 1904. He went down to the edge of the river and waited for Charlie Stratton and Charlie Derby to row over from Highlands, by prearrangement, and take him back into town. Wasson's aim was to enjoy himself with a few drinks, perhaps rendezvous with a few of the spirited Highlands girls and then buy enough liquor for himself and his soldier friends isolated back on post at Fort Hancock. Such had been the customary arrangement for some time and usually caused no special notice by either the military or civilian authorities. The hotel owners and barmen benefited from the lucrative profits, especially in the slow winter season, when few city excursionists frequented the town. Wasson carried lots of cash to pay his water taxi agents, treat them to rounds of drinks and pay the hotel barmen for the many bottles of whiskey that he would bring to his friends back on Sandy Hook.

At about one o'clock on Friday morning, May 13, the locals drinking at Dorsett's hotel sobered the instant they all heard a shot ring out from some place upstairs. It came from the second-floor hallway. Riney Holmes, the barman, sped up the stairs, followed by Ed Dorsett, the proprietor. A man was found lying on the floor, his friend Charlie Derby standing over him, watching as blood gushed from a bullet wound onto the carpet. Charles Stratton was unconscious. They sent someone from the barroom below to get Dr. Andrew from town. He arrived just too late. Besides, no medical attention would have proved beneficial given the nature of the bullet wound. Charles Stratton died within ten minutes. There was a murderer to be apprehended.

Dr. Andrew summoned his father, Dr. R.G. Andrew Sr., a physician in Navesink and also the Monmouth County coroner. He ordered the body taken to the Posten Funeral Parlor in Atlantic Highlands, where the two physicians performed an autopsy on the murder victim that Friday. They determined that the bullet struck Stratton above the left eye and that when it entered, a piece of it was shaved off by contact with a bone and the fragment went out the top of the victim's head. The rest of the bullet went diagonally through the head and fractured the back of the skull but did not exit.

Next, the coroner began his inquest into the murder that afternoon, and it carried over to Monday. The principal and only witness, the only eyewitness besides the killer, was Charles Derby. Under careful and close interrogation, Derby's testimony was somewhat self-contradictory, yet for the most part he clung to the story that he and Stratton had gone to the Dorsett Hotel only in order to get away from Wasson. He admitted that initially they intended to row the soldier back to Sandy Hook, but later on in the evening they took it into their minds to "shake" him. He gave no other details and insisted that they did nothing to provoke Wasson. When they came to the hotel, he said, he and Stratton ran around to the back and went up the rear staircase in their attempt to elude Wasson. The soldier, however, entered by a front staircase, and when they met face to face at the top of the stairs, Wasson drew his revolver and fired one shot at Stratton. Derby said Wasson fled down the back stairs as the people from the bar were coming up the front steps. Derby was pressed to explain why they went to the hotel rather than to their homes if they wanted to "shake" the soldier. In reply, he said that they were familiar with the hotel and that it was closer than home and more convenient to go there.

The murderer ran from the hotel down to the bridge, which he crossed and then entered Highland Beach. From there, he ran to the guard at the south end of the trestle, which he carefully crossed and took up his post at the north end, awaiting to be relieved by the replacement guard. Wasson was arrested inside Fort Hancock on Friday morning and was taken to the county jail.

The state charged George Wasson with murder in the second degree at the arraignment on July 7, 1904. Represented by able counsel, he entered a plea of not guilty. He would claim that he acted in self-defense,

The Fort Hancock guardhouse on Sandy Hook was where Private George Wasson was held in the secure lockup after his murder of Charlie Stratton in Highlands. *Courtesy Tom Hoffman, historian, Gateway National Recreational Area, Sandy Hook.*

being caught up in a threatening situation. The defendant returned to the county lockup, while Charles Derby was held as a material witness on $300 bail and released.

During the trial, Wasson's attorneys laid the groundwork of their self-defense theory. They maintained that Wasson, like many of the Fort Hancock soldiers, was wary of being caught up in a doubly criminal activity in Highlands. Soldiers who went to Highlands without leave, using Highlands men as paid ferrymen and carrying considerable amounts of cash to buy liquor in the several hotels for other men on the post, could find themselves assaulted, held up and robbed by local toughs and left stranded without the agreed-on and paid boat transportation back to Sandy Hook. They could make no report or complaint of the assault and theft either to their officers at the fort or to the police in town, for they had deserted their assigned posts and were subject to court-martial if the facts of their activity became known. They did complain to the men in the barracks about their mistreatment at the hands of the Highlanders. They warned one another who to watch out for.

Charles Stratton had been involved in illegal activity for some time. Lots of people in town knew of it, and some even sympathized with him and those of similar character. Once Stratton had got himself locked up in the town jail, charged with atrocious assault and battery on James Vanderberg, of Highlands, having shot the man in the face with a cannon! He had been there just less than a day when it was discovered that he had somehow escaped. Clearly it was done with inside help, and all policemen, marshals and borough officials who had keys to the lockup were questioned. At the end of the investigation, police arrested Edward Worth for assisting in the prisoner's escape. But within just a few hours, on August 13, 1903, Charles Stratton was apprehended hiding out in a second-floor room at Dorsett's hotel, his hangout, and was handcuffed and transported to the county jail in Freehold. The outcome of the charge and the welfare of the man shot with the cannon are not known. Edward Worth's tombstone has no date of death inscribed.

Charles Stratton had a bad example to follow in his father, Charles Stratton Sr., who had spent five months in the Monmouth County jail, convicted of having broken into two wealthy Rumson homes and stolen expensive goods during the off season in 1894. He did not learn his lesson, for in July 1918 he and a dimwitted partner named Joseph Matthews were arrested and held on $500 bail for giving liquor to and taking sexual advantage of two sixteen-year-old Highlands girls named Marie Robertson and Jennie Holmes.

The trial began on Monday, January 16, 1904, in the Monmouth County Court of Oyer and Terminer in Freehold. Little time was taken the first day in examining and selecting a jury, as well as with the opening remarks by both the state and the defense. The following jurors were accepted without any challenge: Lewis S. Packard (foreman), Garrett Thorne, George Smith, William F. Erickson, Tunis V. Hendrickson, William F. Sherman, William Magahan, Frederick Shocks Jr., Christopher Zeigler, John D. Thompson Jr., Thomas Burns and J. Lloyd Ely. None of these men resided within ten miles of the scene of the crime.

The case for the state was presented by Henry M. Nevius, Monmouth County prosecutor, along with A.J. Stokes, assistant prosecutor. The defense was argued by Attorneys Isaac P. Runyon, E.W. Arrowsmith and Edmund Wilson.

The remainder of Monday morning was devoted to examination of witnesses for both sides. Nevius called eleven witnesses, of whom Charles Derby was the principal one. The two physicians, Dr. Russell G. Andrew Jr. and Dr. Russell G. Andrew Sr., the Monmouth County coroner, gave clinically graphic testimony. The murdered man's wife, Lucinda Stratton, was called to testify. Her two small, fatherless children, Emma (age eleven) and Garrott (eight), were in court the whole time, no doubt to prey on the emotions of the jurors. Others called were the barman Cyrenius Holmes and other bar patrons at the time of the shooting: Frank Osborn, James Riddle, Walter Skidmore, C. Mel Johnson (proprietor of the Seaside Hotel and tavern located at Bay Avenue and Miller Street) and William Waller. All were called simply to show that a killing had taken place at the hotel and to tie Wasson to the other two men. Charles Derby related all of the details from the time they picked Wasson up through to the shooting. He maintained that no threats against Wasson were ever made and that they did not assault or rob him but simply wanted to separate themselves from him. Under cross-examination, however, he admitted that there had been a quarrel between Stratton and Wasson on the way to Dorsett's and that this was the reason for their wanting to "shake" him.

Prosecutor Nevius laid great emphasis on the inconsistencies found in Wasson's statements after his arrest and during trial—for example, he stated at one time that he entered the hotel by the front door and then at another time that he had gone in by the back door. The county detective, Charles E. Strong, who escorted Wasson to Freehold following the coroner's inquest, testified that Wasson claimed that Stratton and Derby had robbed him of twenty-eight dollars. The state rested its case a little after noon on Monday.

The case for the defendant was taken up immediately. The defense list of witnesses included men and women from the bar the night of the shooting or who could give positive character reference testimony in Wasson's favor: Phineus

Burdge, Mahlon Burdge, Otha Johnson, Wright Smith, Silas Emery, Michael Donald, Joseph Stapleton, Mary Babbitt and Edward Dorsett and his wife, Ella. The last and most startling witness called was George Wasson himself.

The "prisoner" (the common reference used for the defendant, which today is considered prejudicial) testified that he had gone to Highlands for a few beers and had fallen in with Stratton and Derby. They did some serious drinking at Murphy's hotel and left there at about eleven o'clock at night for Dorsett's place. On the way there, Derby lashed out at him and accused him of having told Dorsett that Derby had "knocked down" money while tending bar there. Derby then grabbed him by the throat. They told him that they would "fix" him. Wasson escaped away and ran to Dorsett's hotel to get away from the two men, saying that he feared for his life. He went to the Dorsett Hotel to seek refuge in a second-floor room with which he was familiar. He found the door locked. Meanwhile, he heard Derby and Stratton come in the rear door and up the stairs and say, "If he is in the room, we will smash the door." Wasson was crouched behind a banister with his gun drawn. He said that he fired his revolver with the intention of frightening the two men off. He heard a moan. Next, he heard Derby shout, "You have shot Charlie!" Wasson said, "My God, it can't be true!" He denied that he had told detective Strong that the two had robbed him.

Both Ed and Ella Dorsett testified that they had been asleep in their second-floor room and that they were awakened by voices. They said that they heard a voice say, "Let us break the door in."

In the summations given early Tuesday morning, Edmund Wilson for the defense asked that the jury acquit Wasson on the grounds that he had shot Stratton without intent to injure him and in self-defense. Prosecutor Nevius urged the jury to follow the evidence leading them to a conviction, not of murder in the first degree but rather of a lesser level of crime. Judge Dixon instructed the jurors that they could not find the prisoner guilty of first-degree murder and sent them off into the jury room to deliberate Wasson's fate.

The twelve men were retired just a very brief time, less than half an hour, when they returned. The judge asked them if they had reached a verdict. The foreman assured him that they had, and the verdict paper was shown to the judge. He instructed the accused Wasson to stand as the jury foreman read aloud their verdict: guilty of manslaughter. The jury was thanked by Judge Dixon and dismissed. He set sentencing for the next day.

On June 18, 1905, George H. Wasson again stood before Judge Dixon as his sentence was read: "[T]o be imprisoned in state prison at Trenton for ten years at hard labor and from thence until the costs of prosecution are paid."

Life in Highlands fairly well returned to normal—that is, normal for Highlands but abnormal for other towns. Except for poor widow Stratton, now left with two young ones to bring up without their father, who was buried the Sunday following the killing. She had already been struggling financially and had to take her children and live with her mother, Mrs. Electra Layton, a widow since her husband, Aaron, had died years before, in her house with her adult brothers and old man Thomas Parker, a boarder. Stratton worked with Old Lady Layton, taking in wash for the wealthy people living up on the hills far above lower Highlands. When summer came and the crowds of city folk filled the hotels and boardinghouses throughout the town, there would be lots more money coming in and, of course, much more backbreaking work. She was seldom glancing into a mirror, realizing that she was quickly looking much older than her thirty-four years and in little time would seem as old as her mother.

Life was anything but normal for Edward and Ella Dorsett as well. They did not receive renewal of their hotel license from the borough. They themselves could continue to reside there, if they wished, but renting out rooms was not allowed. The county refused to continue their tavern license. Both actions were due as a result of the murder, primarily, but also because at the time of the killing they were under orders, issued the previous day, not to be open to the public, to maintain closed and locked doors and not to operate the bar. They had been accused of running a disorderly house. Rumors went around that they permitted drunkenness, gambling, Sunday liquor sales and illicit sexual relations in their rooms.

Such activity proved to be almost a perennial problem for the town in its early days as an independent borough, as one can see from the following local newspaper clipping:

Red Bank Register
September 26, 1906

Albert and James Hartsgrove of the Highlands were tried and acquitted of keeping a disorderly house at that place. A number of witnesses testified that the house was kept as a disorderly house but their testimony was weak. Immediately after the jury returned with the verdict of "not guilty," Albert Hartsgrove and Belle Robinson, a woman who was alleged to have been one of the inmates of the house, were arrested and held for the action of the October Grand Jury.

All of the adverse publicity generated by the murder and trial was not good for business. The businessmen in town were worried. They thought that business in the summer following the murder in May 1904 was down—perhaps because of the murder and perhaps because of less than ideal weather. No one could be certain. Peter Cornwell, mayor in the Borough of Highlands' fourth year, was concerned by what outsiders were supposedly saying about the town, disparaging comments such as, "What can you expect of the place? Clammers, gamblers, shacks, lawlessness, Sunday drunkenness, and worse yet. The Highlands will always be the Highlands." Mayor Cornwell was worried, and with good reason. Outsiders who had opposed the incorporation of the Borough of Highlands from its beginning on March 22, 1900, no doubt were gloating in their criticism, replete with "I told you so" attitudes, as they read through the following article. Patching up and improving Highlands' reputation proved to be a constant battle for concerned town officials and exasperated spontaneously formed citizens groups:

Red Bank Register
June 27, 1906

DRUNKS MOLEST WOMEN IN WILD AND LAWLESS TOWN
SUNDAY SELLING ENDED
"WIDE OPEN" SUNDAYS ARE OVER
A Law and Order League Is Organized to Compel Observance of the Law—Desirable Guests Are Attracted by the New Order of Things.

The Law and Order League of the Highlands, which was organized about six weeks ago, held a meeting last Wednesday night at Thompson's hotel. The league has more than a hundred members consisting of nearly all the summer residents and all the representative men of the borough. Hal Reid, the playwright, who is a summer cottager, is president of the league and Robert McKay is secretary and treasurer.

Judge John E. Foster had been invited to attend the meeting. His remarks concerned chiefly the powers of the league to preserve order in the community.

The league was in doubt as to whether the borough policemen had a right to make arrests in Ocean township. It was stated that frequently there is more or less disorder on the drawbridge but the two borough officers were averse to making arrests there for fear that it was not within their province to do so. Judge Foster assured the league that the borough officers or any citizen had the power under the statute to arrest any disorderly person. The league will engage another officer for police duty who will serve during the summer.

No complaints were made at the meting. Highlands is said now to be a "dry" town on Sundays. One of the citizens told a Register *reporter on Friday that it was very unlike Sundays in old times, when everything was wide open. Instead of meeting drunken men on all sides, as in former days, there was an air of peaceful quiet about the borough, and women could go where they pleased without being molested or insulted by drunken men.*

This condition of things, it is believed, will attract to the place hundreds of desirable summer guests who in the past have had no desire to take their families to the Highlands on account of the disorder due to its being a wide open place. The indications are that the borough this year will enjoy a big season.

Not long after the Stratton case—just four years later, as a matter of fact—the whole town was buzzing with gossip about another incident, perhaps another case of foul play or even murder committed by those no-good soldiers out there on Sandy Hook. Decent Highlands people were not safe, it was said. Who knows where those army men come from and what they might be running away from.

It was poor Charles Eldridge this time, a waterman, just forty-four years old. Late on Saturday night, May 9, 1908, he took a bunch of soldiers over to the Hook and just never came back:

Red Bank Register
May 27, 1908

Eldridge's Body Found
It Washed Ashore at Sandy Hook Last Saturday
He Had Taken a Party of Soldiers from Highlands to Fort Hancock Two Weeks Ago and Was Never After Seen Alive.

The body of Charles Eldridge of the Highlands, who disappeared from his boat two weeks ago last Saturday, was found on Saturday morning on Sandy Hook by John Ahearn of Belford, foreman of a construction gang who was working on a road near where the body washed ashore. Mr. Eldridge's body had been in the water about two weeks and came ashore near where his boat and hat were found on the morning after his disappearance.

Mr. Eldridge, who was a waterman, started out from Highland Beach late at night to take a party of soldiers to the Horseshoe Dock at Sandy Hook. He never returned and the soldiers were held on suspicion, although they claimed they had paid for their transportation and Mr. Eldridge had started for home in his boat, after he had put them ashore.

Coroner John Tetley of Red Bank was summoned when the body was found, and the body was taken to the Highlands, where it was viewed by the coroner's jury. The body was in very bad condition but it showed no signs of foul play. The body was again examined by Dr. Bennett of Long Branch on Saturday night and he affirmed the first examination that the foul play theory should not be considered.

An inquest will be held tomorrow afternoon at Bernard Creighton's hotel. The coroner's inquest jury is composed of John N. Riker, foreman, Emil Aufieri, Henry Robinson, James Foster, Addison Romaine and Fred Corse. The soldiers are being held to await the action of the coroner and will be taken to the Highlands to testify at the inquest.

Mr. Eldridge was 44 years old. He is survived by his wife, Mrs. Alice Eldridge, and two sons, Howard and Edward, aged thirteen and seven years. He also leaves two sisters and two brothers. They are Mrs. Elizabeth B. Pennent of Bayonne; Mrs. Hattie Voorhees of New Brunswick; George Eldridge of Jersey City and Simeon Eldridge of the Highlands. The Prudential Insurance Co. was to pay his beneficiary $501.62.

The funeral was held from his home yesterday afternoon, Rev. Thomas Huss, pastor of the Highlands Methodist church, having charge of the services. The body was buried at Fair View cemetery.

Following is another article about the Eldridge drowning:

Red Bank Register
June 3, 1908

ACCIDENTAL DROWNING
Verdict of the Coroner's Jury in the Charles Eldridge Case

The inquest in the case of Charles Eldridge, the Highlands fisherman who lost his life under mysterious circumstances a few days ago, was held at Creighton's hotel at the Highlands Thursday afternoon. It was conducted by Coroner John T. Tetley of Red Bank. Eldridge started from the Highlands to take five soldiers to Sandy Hook in his boat. He landed the soldiers in safety, but Eldridge did not show up at Highlands. A search was made and his boat and hat were found. It was then thought that Eldridge had met with foul play and suspicion rested on the soldiers, who were held at the barracks awaiting action of the coroner's inquest.

At the inquest the soldiers testified that they had given Eldridge $2 to take them to Sandy Hook. Corporal Dalton testified that he and two of his companions were perfectly sober, while the other two had been drinking but were able to take care of themselves. He said Eldridge was greatly under the influence of liquor. He testified that he and his companions said good-bye to Eldridge and saw him push his boat into deep water with an oar. That was the last they saw of him. Dalton said he thought Eldridge in his drunken condition may have fallen from his boat into the water and drowned. Eldridge's body was found Saturday and there were no marks of violence. The jury brought in a verdict of accidental drowning.

This was not the last of problems between Fort Hancock soldiers and Highlanders, by any means; they continued for almost as long as Fort Hancock and Highlands remained adjacent to each other.

Sources: *Red Bank Register*, August 1, 1894; November 11, 1903; May 18, 1904; January 18, 1905; June 27, 1906; September 26, 1906; May 27, 1908; June 3, 1908; and July 3, 1918; Monmouth County Archives, Coroner's Reports and Oyer and Terminer Minutes Books.

HIGHLANDS A HUB IN THE RUMRUNNING ERA

This account of the days when rumrunners evaded authorities in and around Highlands to satisfy their customers' desires and to better their own financial gain—all in the face of the prohibition laws—is based on newspaper reports and on the personal reminiscences shared by John "Buddy" Bahrs, former mayor, restaurateur and Highlands native but never a rumrunner.

Bahrs was just a twelve-year-old boy when prohibition became the law nationwide on January 20, 1920. His father had been taking the family from their home in Newark to Highlands to spend the summer since 1912, and one summer he found what he considered a great opportunity: buying a boathouse and boat rental business located on the river at the foot of Cedar Street, where the James T. White Clam Depuration plant stands today. Later, his father, John H. Bahrs, and mother, Florence, bought McGuire's boathouse

John Alvin Bahrs (1908–1998), known to all as "Buddy" or "Bud," was essentially "Mr. Highlands," for the only place he loved. Restaurateur, councilman, mayor and historian, Bahrs was pleased to share his intimate knowledge of Highlands, both the good and the bad.

on the site of today's Bahrs Landing Restaurant, where the whole family moved in. It was a tough life for the mother and kids, living year round in the two-story boathouse that had half a dozen bunks on one floor and some fifty on the other, all with mattresses stuffed with cornstalks and straw. Soon weekend fishermen made Bahrs their headquarters, and the kids (Ruth, Al, Ken and Buddy), sleeping on the hard and cold bunks, made it their home without ever a complaint.

Fishermen used to pay $3.50 each for boat, bait, bunk and board provided by Florence Bahrs's good home cooking, which was served on tables covered with sheet metal. There were no menus, tablecloths or napkins and no complaints, just thanks from the fishermen going for flounder, fluke, porgies, blues and striped bass in the river.

The rumrunners or bootleggers made Highlands their base of illegal operations since it was the nearest New Jersey town to the offshore supply ships and since there were plenty of large, powerful and fast-moving lobster boats (refitted with very powerful war surplus airplane engines) there for easy hire to bring the whiskey contraband around the Hook and into waiting cars and trucks, having outrun any pursuing Coast Guard patrol boats. They chose Bahrs because it was right on the water, close to the ocean and offered warm hospitality, decent accommodations and good food, especially Florence's delicious clam chowder, which is available today in cans and made according to the original recipe.

Wicked Days of Prohibition and Rumrunning

While the buyers were all men from the cities with associations to a tougher criminal element in organized crime, the men who ran the boats were all locals, good seamen, hardworking lobstermen and clammers who saw nothing wrong with their participation in this victimless crime, who had struggled to make ends meet even before the Depression hit and who were legitimized in their unlawfulness by the senselessness of the law that few ever wanted and no one respected. These Highlands men could ride out past the three-mile limit (later nine miles) of U.S. jurisdiction, day or night, in storm or calm, to "Rum Row" off Highlands, Sea Bright, Monmouth Beach and Long Branch, where a small fleet of ships from Canada and Jamaica awaited buyers.

While at first rumrunning boats operated boldly in broad daylight, since initially there was no patrol set up to stop them, soon they had to work under cover of darkness to disguise their crime. The city men would sit around one or more iron stoves in Bahrs—talking, playing cards, even reading—waiting to find out when and where the boats were coming in with their purchases. A lookout on the rocks over at Highland Beach used binoculars and a powerful flashlight to detect and respond to prearranged signals from the boats at Rum Row. Then, shining his beams into Bahrs, he let the men know where to meet the boats—at Highlands, Atlantic Highlands, Leonardo, Belford or someplace else. All of the men jumped up, downed their drinks or coffees and ran to their cars and trucks. They used big and fast Diamond Reo Speed Wagons, but many also preferred long sedans fitted up with extra heavy-duty springs since these had the needed space, the speed and the element of disguise. With fifteen or more cases of Canadian whiskey in the backs of the cars, they could ride to the city looking just like plain, ordinary tourists returning from the shore.

The bootleggers (Whitey, Dutch, Providence and Dingbat were some of the aliases used) who worked through the Bahrs family respected them and their business, were polite (especially to Mrs. Bahrs), treated the kids well and always paid their bills with generosity. However, the respect was not necessarily reciprocated. John Bahrs knew full well that what he was doing was wrong, but it was business and times were tough—he was just starting out, and he had to make a living, as he had a family to feed. Many a local, many a bootlegger, thought that Bahrs should use his large sea skiff for a more lucrative business than the pound-net fishing it had been built for by Seaman Boats in Long Branch. They urged Bahrs to get with it, to wise up and to take the boat out and load it up with whiskey to make "a real dollar or two." He hated what he was already doing. His wife Florence worried about the whole affair. She wanted no part of it, and so Bahrs refused.

The rumrunner sloop *Kirk and Sweeney*, anchored on Rum Row with crates of whiskey waiting for offloading to high-speed lobster and fishing boats from places all along Raritan Bay and Sandy Hook Bay.

It seemed that everyone was into the bootlegging thing, including the officer in charge at the Coast Guard base on Sandy Hook, who would get a telephone call that rum boats were coming into Highlands. He would send his patrol- and gunboats to look in a different location, say, by Perth Amboy. The men would find nothing, but he would find a quarter case of good Canadian waiting on his own dock. Just about everyone in Highlands reaped the benefits of prohibition and rumrunning. They made plenty of fast money and spent it swiftly. The women who worked in the clam shucking and stringing sheds along the river suddenly had fur coats to keep them warm in the bitterly cold huts and homes. Some even glamorously displayed new diamond rings on their fingers, like the movie starlets they saw in the theater there in Highlands, even with fingers like stubs from opening clams.

From time to time, there would be raids on Highlands speakeasies. Police would swoop into several places simultaneously, and the results would be read in the papers the next Thursday (not so much in the *Highlands Star* or the *Atlantic Highlands Journal*, the local town papers), in the *Red Bank Register*, for example, on June 11, 1930: "County detectives made five raids at the

Encrusted bottles like these were what Bill Janus dredged up from the bay floor. At times of severe low tide, Highlands kids used to walk out to Sandy Hook, picking up perfectly good bottles of whiskey and selling them for fifty cents to local bars.

Highlands. The owners of the places were arraigned in Freehold and held in $1,000 bail for the Grand Jury on charges of illegal possession and sale. Arrested were Tom Caioli, Emil Aufieri, S. Wilson, Michael Mendes, and Frank Mulligan." Apparently, it was without public shame or disapproval that they remained in town, using their profits to finance memorial windows in the new church being built and opening legal taverns after prohibition was over.

The glamour evaporated, the money devalued and the thrills vanished whenever a bootlegging affair went contrary to expectations. Coast Guard machine gun bullets ripped open a man's spine in a boat headed for shore, and he died sprawled on the floor of the sedan intended for whiskey. A man was blinded for life in an explosion when he poured naphtha instead of gasoline into a hot boat engine to make it run faster when being pursued.

When the Twenty-first Amendment to the Constitution repealed the Eighteenth Amendment, national prohibition came to an end on December 5, 1933. The lobstermen returned to their lobster pots, the clammers to their boats, bushels and rakes and people to the twenty-six taverns licensed in the little borough of Highlands, just 0.64 square mile in size.

BOOZE BURIES ITS VICTIM ON SANDY HOOK

Private Isidore Dunsky of the Seventh Coast Artillery Regiment, stationed at Fort Hancock, was listed as AWOL (absent without official leave) on December 20, 1924. He was not considered a deserter since he had left behind $152 cash in his footlocker, as well as a bank book showing a deposit of $2,005, besides civilian clothing and assorted personal possessions. Dunsky had recently purchased a home for his parents at 2274 Douglas Street, Brooklyn, and had left them about $20,000. Mr. and Mrs. Dunsky stated that their son had earned this money by making loans to other soldiers and by outside business ventures, notably a cobbler's business.

Dunsky's body was discovered on February 12, 1925, buried in a shallow grave at Spermaceti Cove on Sandy Hook. It had been found by a party composed of a Coast Guardsman, a Fort Hancock officer and about ten soldiers, all of whom had formed a party searching the sands along the bay for "buried treasure" (i.e., illegal whiskey dumped and concealed by rumrunners being pursued by Coast Guard authorities). This was a common bootlegger practice; otherwise, they used to throw their contraband whiskey, pure Canadian and Scotch whiskey, overboard, thus ditching the incriminating evidence and making their boats lighter and faster for escape.

Sandy Hook's Spermaceti Cove, so named when such whales were common in the area, was the scene of Isidore Dunsky's murder and burial. It has always been a beautiful and remote area and is now a wildlife refuge in Gateway National Recreational Area, Sandy Hook.

Dunsky had been shot three times, once in the head and twice in the torso. Gunpowder residue found on his face and chest showed that he had been shot at close range while standing and facing his killer. The grave was shallow (about thirty inches deep) and hastily arranged, located about 500 feet from the water and 150 feet from an old army utility building in an area with overgrown brush and grass. Dunsky had been killed wearing his fatigue uniform, and his bloodstained hat was at his side. He was placed into the grave on his back, with his knees slightly pulled up to his chest. Rusty cans and scrap iron were scattered about the grave and may have been used in an attempt to disguise it.

There was a jurisdictional dispute between the Monmouth County prosecutor, Charles F. Sexton, and the military authorities on Fort Hancock—Colonel Elijah B. Martindale Jr., post commandant, and Executive Officer Colonel H.J. Watson.

Journalists were barred by the military from learning the names of the men in the party that came upon the grave and also from interviewing them. However, the Coast Guardsman, whose name was kept secret by the press, was interviewed and quoted by a reporter from the *New York Times* in an article dated February 15, 1925.

A formal military board of inquiry was convened to investigate the case, but after taking statements from the officer and enlisted men and visiting the grave, the members adjourned, awaiting possible future evidence and witnesses regarding Dunsky's killer or killers.

The Fort Hancock barracks for enlisted men, where Isidore Dunsky ran a big money operation by making loans to other soldiers and also through outside business ventures—a cobbler's business (according to his parents) and a whiskey business for soldiers (according to authorities). *Courtesy Tom Hoffman, historian, Gateway National Recreational Area, Sandy Hook.*

Theories, however, abounded. Isidore Dunsky had been engaged in criminal moneymaking activities. The amount of cash he had at his disposal and the location of the murder suggested that he was involved in some aspect of rumrunning. Likely he had been dealing with civilian rumrunners or had made or agreed to make purchases of whiskey (doubly illegal: once in the whole United States and once on a military reservation) for sale and distribution to officers and soldiers on Fort Hancock. He likely had known the men who killed him, met them along Spermaceti Cove and was thought to have somehow cheated them. It is likely that Dunsky, in cooperation with his rumrunning cohorts, had hidden his cache of whiskey in the sands of Spermaceti Cove, an out-of-the-way location, and that the Fort Hancock men who stumbled upon the body had suspected that Dunsky had hidden his whiskey supplies there.

Afterward, Private Isidore Dunsky's body was taken from Fort Hancock on February 14, 1925. The post flag was at half mast, and an honor guard of soldiers armed with rifles escorted the body to an awaiting army tugboat as a trumpet sounded. Under the command of Lieutenant George Savini, they sailed to the army pier at Fifty-eighth Street, Brooklyn. As the tug crossed the open water of the lower bay, the men aboard stared in awe as they watched a Coast Guard cutter fire several rounds at fleeing rumrunning boats loaded with whiskey. The funeral was held at the home of the dead soldier's parents, and burial took place at Montefiore Cemetery, Queens.

Thrilling Detective, one of the most popular dime magazines of the time, published the story "Sandy Hook Murders," a so-called book-length novel supposedly written by Lieutenant John Hopper, in its August 1932 issue. The Dunsky murder case was the inspiration for this thrilling work.

RUMRUNNING RISKS: FAMILY MAN KILLED FOR BOOZE PROFIT

What took place in the early hours of July 2, 1924, on the ocean just east of Sandy Hook, but out of the sight of land, might have been the makings of a novel of swashbuckling pirate adventure on the high seas had it not taken on the grim reality of death and destruction. There was a high-speed pursuit of bootleggers in fast lobster boats with high-powered engines, outmaneuvering and outrunning the more cumbersome Coast Guard patrol boats.

Gerard Kadenbach—called Gerry by every friendly face in booze-infested Highlands during the long, torturous years of national prohibition—paid the price, either justified or unjustified, while just trying to make a buck or two moving whiskey from sailing ships far off shore to middlemen waiting on land. Kadenbach paid with his life.

One shot rang out in the ocean silence splintered by the whine of engines opened wide at full throttle. Young Kadenbach slumped over the boat's controls, bringing the craft to a stop. His spine had been ripped open like a zipper by the single large-caliber bullet that tore into his torso near his lungs. There was blood everywhere. Yet there was no illegal liquor found aboard the boat. Some said that was because he had dumped the Canadian cargo to destroy the evidence in case he was apprehended. They also said that there was no lobster gear or other fishing equipment found on board.

Captain Tilton was in charge of the cutter *Gresham* and of the crewman who fired the fatal shot. It was not known whether the captain had ordered his men to fire, and further investigation by Monmouth County detective John M. Smith was cut short by Coast Guard district superintendent Samuel Nichols, who claimed that the affair had become a U.S. Department of Justice matter.

The men in the lobster boats who first rendered Kadenbach assistance lashed out against the brutality of the Coast Guard, claiming that Kadenbach had done nothing wrong, had no booze on board, had fled the Coast Guard craft out of fear and clearly had been out on the water for purely innocent purposes, perhaps just for boating pleasure. The Coast Guard had pursued two boats, one belonging to the injured man and the other likely belonging to one of the so-called lobstermen, who had no lobsters, not many lobsterpots and, of course, no illegal liquor on board.

Initially, the cutter took the wounded Kadenbach on board, but once it was determined that he needed more than just first-aid treatment, they returned him, as bad off as he was from shock and loss of blood, to his own boat. A lobsterman came aboard and raced at high speed, piloting the boat to the beach nearest the Long Branch Hospital. Some five hours after the shot was fired, though somewhat conscious all the while, Gerard Kadenbach succumbed to his wound.

Kadenbach was just twenty-four years old, the husband of the former Dena Layton, the father of little baby Ida (just two months old) and the son of Gerard Kadenbach, proprietor of the well-known Kadenbach's Hardware of Bay Avenue, Highlands. He left behind two sisters, Helen and Monica, and a brother, Gothard.

Gerard Kadenbach's funeral was largely attended at his father's house under the direction of Reverend Harry P. Grim of the Methodist Church. Burial took place at the Fair View Cemetery.

Practically the whole town turned out to attend the solemn affair and to offer Mr. Kadenbach their sympathies and condolences. It had a somber and dulling effect on every Highlander, coming as it did just at the big celebration for the Fourth of July. Despite it all, men soon returned to the ocean in high-speed boats, awaiting the next shipment of whiskey to make themselves some fast and easy money as rumrunners.

RUMRUNNER SHOOTOUT IN THE HEART OF ATLANTIC HIGHLANDS

One man was murdered, six or more were wounded and several men were locked up in jail. These were the results of a major gunfight on Saturday night, September 21, 1923, at Atlantic Highlands between bootleggers and hijackers. These were rum pirates who made a business of holding up bootleggers and stealing their "wet goods."

Frank LeConte of Newark, who was said to have been the king of the hijacking gangs, was the man killed, having died the following Monday morning at the Long Branch Hospital. He and a gang of other Newark men had been at the Highlands in an automobile, and when they left that town, they were followed by another car filled with Highlands men, under the leadership of Robert Schneider.

People in the know about such matters stated that the shootout had been caused by a grudge of several months' standing. Various stories circulated concerning the cause of the dispute. The one most credited was that the Highlanders had been stopped the previous summer by Newark hijackers, while the Highlands men were in an automobile filled with booze. Not only did the Newark men take the whiskey, but they also gave the Highlands men a severe beating.

The two rival gangs fought it out with guns in Atlantic Highlands that Saturday night, just a stone's throw from the railroad station and First Avenue on Center Avenue, an area typically thick with day visitors and shoppers. When the Newark gang left the Highlands in a large Cadillac, they were followed by their enemies. They sped out of Highlands at a fast clip, up along Navesink Avenue, down Buttermilk Valley and along Valley Drive, until they turned sharp onto First Avenue, the town's main business street. Next, they swerved left onto Center Avenue and came to a screeching halt as the crossing gates came down for a passing train. The Newark men jumped out of their car and took cover behind trees, poles and buildings. Simultaneously, shots flew in every direction from both sides.

It was reminiscent of the accounts of shootouts in the streets of Dodge City during the heyday of lawlessness in the Old West. It started at about ten o'clock, while the Saturday night crowd was finishing up its shopping. There was still a considerable number of innocent pedestrians in the business section, heading for the station or their parked automobiles near the railroad. Everyone headed for cover, ducking into cars, houses and shops. Some crouched behind barrels and horse water troughs. All kept their heads down low to avoid getting killed or becoming witnesses against these ruthless criminals.

LeConte fell early in the gunplay, getting struck near a tree just about opposite the town hall/firehouse. The bullet hit him in the stomach, broke his belt buckle and passed through his body, finally being trapped beneath the skin on his back. The town mayor and respected physician Dr. Harry A. Henrickson treated LeConte in his office after he was scooped up and carried there by his gang members, who abandoned him there.

The gravely wounded LeConte at first refused to give his name and address to the doctor and the police. Finally, in the Long Branch Hospital, after being assured that his wounds were likely to prove fatal, he surrendered that information but steadfastly refused to name any of his fellow gang members. He only kept saying that he had plenty of money in his pockets and that he would pay well for the best medical attention. Despite all of the efforts of the doctors, Frank LeConte died on Monday morning, September 23, 1923.

Those arrested in the hours following the shootout were John Butterfield and Henry and George Nettinger of Highlands, as well as Alfred Buckmeister. Further, Walter Keener, Ralph and Edward Bitters and Joseph LeConte, brother of the murdered man, were apprehended by county detective Jacob Rue. Robert Schneider was taken in by county detective John Smith and two state troopers in Sea Bright.

Ralph Bitters had been wounded early in the onslaught but was able to keep on shooting. Most of the men in both gangs received slight wounds but had avoided seeking medical attention for fear of being arrested.

The rumrunner battle worked the decent people of Atlantic Highlands into a worried frenzy, and so they were living day to day in a state of high anxiety bordering on terror. People said that they did not know what to expect next from the criminal elements, fearing that a gunfight could erupt at any time. They were so panicked that they refused to leave their homes after dark.

One indication of the dreadful state of Atlantic Highlands affairs was mentioned by a resident who spoke only on the condition of anonymity. A short time ago, he said, the home of William Jennings, former president

William Jennings's home on Second Avenue, Atlantic Highlands, shows the disarray that he used as his defense that he simply forgot about the four hundred cases of whiskey that authorities found there, claiming it was pre-prohibition booze. *Courtesy Randall Gabrielan, Monmouth County historian.*

of the borough council, was raided by federal men, the "dry agents," who confiscated a large lot of illegal whiskey.

Mayor Hendrickson said that since the start of prohibition, towns that once had been filled with good, God-fearing residents now were being infiltrated and taken over by criminal elements from the big cities to the north, joining with the same element already living in places like Highlands and Atlantic Highlands, all attracted by the lure of fast, easy money in bootlegging, which so many folk considered a victimless crime.

Not a single gangster arrested could be forced to testify against either a fellow gang member or even an enemy gang member. Since it was dark, there were no witnesses besides the shooters, and it was impossible to prove who owned the pistol that fired the bullet that murdered LeConte. No charges were brought against anyone. No one arrested spent time in jail, as they all had pocketfuls of money, sometimes as much as $5,000, used to post bail.

BRIEF NEWS ARTICLES ON RUMRUNNING IN THE HIGHLANDS

Town Councilman Charged with Bootlegging

William Jennings, once a respected member of the Atlantic Highlands Borough Council under Mayor Harry Hendrickson, was forced to resign his position in disgrace. In late 1922, prohibition agents found four hundred cases of whiskey in his cellar. Jennings first claimed that the booze had been there from before the start of prohibition and that he had forgotten about it. Later, he maintained that the contraband was not his and that he did not know it had been in the cellar, which he rarely entered. The mayor and council members were not persuaded and demanded his resignation.

Worse was yet to come for Jennings. On the night of November 30, 1923, Jennings was on the beach at Wagner's Creek on the western border of Atlantic Highlands when New Jersey state troopers seized forty cases of whiskey. The wide-mouthed creek, with easy access for cars and trucks, was a common and protected spot for small boats to discharge their contraband picked up from the supply ships on Rum Row. In that week alone, police had seized 327 cases at the creek.

Trooper Harley Hutchinson saw a group of men near the cases as he reached the beach. He called to them to freeze and not make a move to get away. Jennings turned, stopped and started to reach into his hip pocket. Hutchinson drew his revolver and fired one shot, striking Jennings in the leg. He fell to the ground when the bullet splintered the thigh bone. He was given aid by the other men and the trooper and remained quite conscious. He was placed under arrest along with the others and questioned; then he was rushed in a police car to the hospital in Long Branch.

Jennings and the rest maintained that they knew nothing of the booze, having only heard a report that it was sitting there on the beach, and out of innocent curiosity, they went to the creek to just look at the whiskey. This did not deter the police. Then Jennings said that he had supper in a home near the creek and was just hanging around there for his father to come and pick him up and drive home.

William Jennings stopped worrying about getting arrested, being prosecuted or fined. He had more urgent concerns. The pain he suffered grew intense. Doctors immediately operated to save his leg, but to no avail. Blood poisoning and infections overwhelmed their efforts, as there were no antibiotics in 1923. Surgeons amputated his leg in a final attempt to save his life. Despite all this, William Jennings died on December 31, 1923, at age forty-one.

Sources: *Red Bank Register*, December 5, 1923; and January 2, 1924; *New York Times*, December 1, 1923.

Grocers and Wanton Women Provision Boats in the Rum Fleet

Each week, scores of boaters sailed from town out around Sandy Hook and into the ocean to Rum Row, originally three miles and later nine miles outside United States territorial waters. Most made the trip under the cover of darkness and without lights on their craft, a potentially disastrous operation. These were the rumrunners looking to buy as many cases of whiskey as they could afford and could carry safely back to shore and to awaiting trucks and heavy sedans.

However, not every boat made the trip out to Rum Row for whiskey. Some boats were even filled to the gunnels on the trip out, returning home to Highlands rather empty.

The ships waiting in Rum Row, steamships or sailing vessels, typically came from quite distant places: from Jamaica and Cuba with rum and from Scotland and Canada with whiskey. Like huge seagoing warehouses crammed with rum and whiskey, a Rum Row ship would spend sometimes as much as five months satisfying the illegal and burning desire for alcohol on the part of the majority of American people.

The crews aboard these ships sometimes ran out of coal for the boilers in order to provide light, heat and passage back home. Sometimes they were in need of fresh water for drinking, cooking and bathing. At times, the ship's cook needed fresh meat, flour, butter, milk, eggs and vegetables. There was a regular fleet of small boats, called "provision boats," that left Highlands and Atlantic Highlands with groceries, coal and kerosene to fill orders placed via word of mouth by rumrunners returning to town. This profitable work was safe and all quite legal.

On occasion, the crews on the Rum Row ships had other needs to be met, especially after they had been at sea so long that they imagined seeing lovely, topless mermaids beckoning from the waves. The "provision boats" provided women—not local girls, of course, but rather from towns like Long Branch and Asbury Park—for short stays at sea. They loved the sea air and swore that it improved their complexions.

Rumrunners by Any Other Name

The members of the Ladies Temperance Union on First Avenue in Atlantic Highlands were just too polite to use bad language and names to describe all of the rumrunners brazenly operating in their town. In hushed voices, they called them outlaws, rumrunners, lawbreakers, disturbers of the peace, bootleggers, brigands, pirates, criminals and perhaps un-Christian men.

The language the state troopers, Monmouth County detectives, local policemen and Coast Guardsmen used for these same men—especially when they let loose with high-power rifle and even machine volleys on the prohibition enforcers pursuing them—is best left unwritten and unspoken.

The prohibition criminals themselves, when caught in the act with or without a boatload of booze, were fond of calling themselves "bottle fishermen," "whiskey fishermen," "servers of the public will," "rum marines," "sport fishermen" and even "sightseers." Those who became really wealthy in the illegal operation became "rum barons."

Two Highlands men, caught and arrested by U.S. Customs agents, defended themselves, saying that they had never, and would never, break the law by running illegal whiskey to Highlands from the ships anchored in Rum Row. They explained to the magistrate that they were only laborers earning a fair wage by loading cases of whiskey from a Canadian ship onto a sailing sloop or high-speed boat. The outcome for William Bush and Harold Eldridge in court is not known.

The term "bootlegger" first appeared in the 1920s at the start of prohibition. It is thought to refer to the concealment of flasks of illegal whiskey in high rubber boots, typical of a fisherman's or lobsterman's work boots.

Sources: *Red Bank Register* and *New York Times*, throughout 1920–33.

Rumrunners Complain to the Police

It is hard to understand the audacity, or the stupidity, of two area men who had their contraband whiskey stolen by six thugs—rough-looking blokes, all heavily armed with revolvers. They entered police headquarters to report the robbery. Charlie Kruger and Sam Foster claimed that they were innocent chauffeurs of the Arrow Transport Company. In their report, they estimated the value of the stolen whiskey at $1,500 and the value of the truck at $400. The police chief did not take their complaint seriously; he suspected that the two had actually sold the booze locally, pocketed the money and then used the alleged robbery to satisfy their boss at the trucking company.

Source: *Atlantic Highlands Journal*, May 16, 1923.

A Highlands Fisherman's Luck

William Janus of Atlantic Highlands had been a fisherman working the local waters all his life. People knew it, too, from the weathered look of the hide on his face and arms. He himself knew it from the nearly constant ache in his back and across his shoulders. It was a hard life, and as much as he loved it, he dreamed of striking it rich, pulling up a trophy-sized striped bass or, better, in his wildest musings, pulling up a small chest of gold and gems. Maybe Captain Kidd's treasure!

His luck with the fish had never been better than mediocre. Still, he had paid off the cost of his thirty-foot sloop and provided well enough for his wife and kids. Janus was dragging the bottom for crabs and hauling in meager numbers. He figured that he would make one last sweep and call it quits. It was a cold day on Thursday, January 24, 1929, and he wished that he had something to soothe his anxiety and to warm his insides, something that was not hot tea or clam broth.

In his drag net, he discovered a bottle of Canadian Club whiskey, with the cork intact and covered with encrustations of barnacles. He knew that it must have been part of contraband dumped over the side of a rumrunner's boat in order to lighten the craft. At other times, the bootleggers just jettisoned the evidence before being overtaken and boarded by the "dry agents." He made another pass over the same area and came up with sixteen bottles of booze. He could not believe his good luck.

Just then, as if out of nowhere, a customs boat swept in. Men boarded the sloop, spotted the contraband goods and took them and William Janus to New York to answer for his very bad luck.

Source: *New York Times*, January 26, 1929.

Famous Highlands Hotel Owner Sued by Scottish Distillery

During prohibition, illegal operations of various sorts were carried out right under the noses of police authorities, often right in the town of Highlands.

The Conners Cedar Grove Hotel was built in 1907 by William H. Conners on swampland cleared, filled and planted by Conners himself. His daughter, Marie, married Herman Black, who with his sons ran the well-known resort, razed for parking for Seastreak ferries to Manhattan.

In the Water Witch section of Highlands, the Conners Cedar Grove Hotel had been an extremely popular resort, especially in the summer for couples and families wanting to escape the stifling heat of the cities to the north. Prohibition created especially difficult times for the hotel, to such an extent that Herman Black, who had married Marie Conners, the founder's daughter, felt compelled to have alcohol for his guests to enjoy and to get whiskey in the most economical and least dangerous manner possible.

Black actually went to the main source of good booze: he traveled to Halifax, Nova Scotia, Canada, where the possession, use and sale of alcoholic beverages was not against the law, as it was throughout the United States. On October 2, 1925, he contracted with C. Levine and Company, of Glasgow, Scotland, for 3,000 cases of Black Rod scotch whiskey at ten dollars per case and 110 cases of Diamond scotch at four dollars per case. Black received on credit the shipment of whiskey aboard his boat, the *C.S. Dorin*, there in Halifax, after actually paying sixty cents per case as a delivery charge.

By December 1927, Herman Black had the cargo moved to St. Pierre, an island to the north of Nova Scotia and technically part of France. It was from here that periodic shipments were made down the Atlantic coast, into Sandy Hook Bay and onto the beach at the Conners Cedar Grove Hotel.

Whiskey sales at Rum Row were done in cash on the spot; however, somehow Herman Black, perhaps as head of an established and well-known New Jersey resort, was trusted to receive the whiskey on credit there in Halifax. Unfortunately for C. Levine and Company, Black paid it not even one Canadian cent. Twenty-two telegrams and letters later, all ignored, a New York Supreme Court justice signed an order for all law agencies to seize any and all of the possessions of Herman Black and the Conners Cedar Grove to satisfy the judgment.

Source: *New York Times*, September 13, 1928.

Part IV

Murders—Some Tragic, Some Comic, All Wicked

A Terribly Tragic Tale of Failed Romance and Revenge

Not in anyone's memory had there ever been such a huge and universal outpouring of grief and sympathy in Atlantic Highlands. St. Agnes Church was not large enough to receive all of the hundreds of mourners the morning of the High Solemn Requiem Mass celebrated by the pastor Reverend Michael H. Callihan. After the service, the priest even delivered a brief sermon to all those unable to enter who were gathered outside the church. He spoke in kindly words, melodic in their Irish tones and phrasing, how all must strive to live life always prepared for heaven's call, knowing neither the day nor the hour of our death on this earth. He held up Mary Agnes Linzmayer, the deceased, as an example for the life of all, calling her a sweet angel of a girl brought into the loving arms of Jesus long before family, relatives, friends and fellow workers thought fitting.

Mary Agnes's end came in the dark, in an automobile parked on a deserted road, on the night of July 10, 1925. There was a muffled scream, followed by two gunshots and flashes that instantaneously illuminated the scene on Ward Avenue, Rumson, New Jersey. Both witnesses to the crime were dead, seated in the front seat of a Dodge sedan. A watchman at an adjacent summer estate fronting on the river, Serge Medvedev, heard the shots, approached the car, saw the situation and summoned help from another home. The Rumson police responded and called county detective Jacob Rue of Red Bank.

According to Rue's investigation and report to the Monmouth County prosecutor, it was a murder-suicide, a tragic tale of failed romance and revenge. The man must have been crazy. He was Henry D. Walling, the married twenty-six-year-old detective sergeant of the Long Branch Police Department, son of William D. Walling, the chief of police there. Linzmayer's friends and fellow workers told Rue that she had known Walling only a very short time, desired nothing more than a casual, friendly relationship with him and knew that he was married, thus precluding him from any romantic relationship with her as a practicing Catholic. Interviews with friends who knew Walling revealed that on more than one occasion he had expressed an infatuation with the girl, that he was on the verge of leaving his wife for her and that, after she attempted to break off the friendship, he would kill her before permitting her to see other men.

Detective Jacob Rue assumed that Mary Agnes had agreed to meet Walling one last time in order to bring the relationship to an end, causing as little pain and hurt as possible for him. He found that Linzmayer had been shot through the heart once, killing her instantaneously, with the bullet lodging near her spine. Walling then turned his service revolver on himself, attempting to shoot through the heart but missing slightly, causing the bullet to pass through his body and into the auto seat upholstery. He did not die instantly but, according to Medvedev, rocked back and forth in his seat behind the steering wheel for a short time before expiring. In so far as Walling had his police hat, blackjack and holster between himself and Mary Agnes, Rue concluded that he had picked her up at the hospital in Long Branch where she worked and drove around for a time.

Mary Agnes Linzmayer was the daughter of Jacob Linzmayer of Atlantic Highlands, of a family with deep roots and many friends in the area. She had just the month before happily celebrated her twenty-second birthday at home and with friends. She had a spotless reputation and was above reproach. Just the previous March, she had graduated from the Long Branch Hospital, Monmouth Memorial Hospital, as a registered nurse. At the exercises, she had received a special fifty-dollar award for proficiency in operating room procedures. She was one of the model students in her class and was held in high esteem by the hospital superintendent, Mrs. Martha Scott, and all her fellow nurses. Shortly after graduation, she was made temporary supervisor of one of the hospital floors.

Actually, Mary Agnes had little time for socializing; she had worked for three months before her death as a private-duty night nurse for a hospital patient, working tirelessly from seven o'clock in the evening to seven o'clock in the morning, always arriving and departing for home with a fellow nurse.

She was a person with a mild, unassuming and easygoing nature whose life was centered on nursing, her friends and family and her church. At her funeral Mass, more than several pews on both sides of the aisle were filled tightly with bright white uniforms and the glistening white starched caps of Long Branch nurses there to honor the memory of Mary Agnes Linzmayer.

Source: *Red Bank Register*, July 15, 1925.

JUST A HORRIBLE LITTLE HOMICIDE AND GREAT WICKEDNESS

Numbers of dead people have been found periodically on the beaches of Sandy Hook and the Highlands for years since the start of the regular running of packet-sloops and steamboats between New York, Long Branch and Red Bank. Monmouth County detectives and coroners always handled these cases with the detachment required to maintain police professionalism and personal good emotional heath.

One particular case, however, moved even the hardened county veterans to the verge of angry tears, when the nude body of a baby girl, just two days old, was found on Tuesday night, May 21, 1906. Two Highlands boys found it floating in the wash of the Shrewsbury River in the sands of Island Beach, just off the town of Highlands. Demarest Newman and Harvey Parker were the two unfortunate lads to come upon the body as they were doing nothing in particular, just exploring and walking around the island. Once they realized what they had found was a baby, they jumped into their boat and rowed faster than ever before over to tell the bridge attendant at the Highlands.

The county coroner, McDonald, and Dr. Riddle of Long Branch arrived and examined the body. The baby had been born alive, without medical attendance, and was perfectly developed, except that the baby's tiny throat had been cut from ear to ear, likely done to silence her cries.

Source: *Red Bank Register*, May 30, 1906.

TORTURE, TERROR AND DEATH ON SANDY HOOK BAY

A Saturday fishing trip in early June for six work buddies should have been a great day of fun. Lots of beer drinking, occasionally interrupted just long enough to catch a fish or two per man, contributed to the good time five of the guys were having. One man, named Mike—the smallest, quietest and least comfortable of all when it came to fishing, boating or just being on the open water—was not really enjoying himself much at all.

They had not let up with name-calling, the kicks in the rear end, both figurative and physical, and the bullying from the minute he climbed into the pickup truck and had to scrunch down behind the two big men in front, Kevin and Tom. In fact, as the day went on their bullying intensified; but the little guy could take it. He had to take it; he had no choice. Where could he go? There he was, almost in the middle of the ocean, and he could not swim.

Such tormenting behavior was normal and tolerated at APA, a trucking company in North Bergen, where five of the six men worked. One was the dispatcher, three were drivers and the last man (the smallest man) was a dockworker and general doer of things no one else wanted to do, like cleaning the toilet and showers and sweeping the locker room. He had been down on his luck for some time before the fishing trip to Sandy Hook. Without family to fall back on when he lost his apartment, as dismal as it was, they let him live as best he could in the company building. They felt sorry for him, but that did not stop them from tormenting him with the incessant name-calling and bullying insults. They laughed, they all laughed, and even he laughed, as if it were all just good-natured kidding around. Their laughter and bullying soon stopped, however, the early afternoon of June 5, 1999.

The party had pulled two boats on trailers down to the Sandy Hook Bay shore to the launching ramps at Atlantic Highlands Municipal Marina at the foot of First Avenue. The big guy, Kevin Kulikowski, twenty-nine, of Secaucus, owned and operated with some skill his 1975 *Galaxy*, a nineteen-foot open cabin outboard. His brother-in-law and best friend, Thomas M. Lyons, thirty-five, of Nutley (or Fort Lee, by some sources) and the little man, Mike Augulis, age thirty-four, were aboard. The other three men were on board a sixteen-foot Crestliner open outboard. They generally kept the two boats close enough to each other so that they could yell back and forth, bragging to and cajoling one another as the day became early afternoon. The wind had picked up a bit and caused just a little chop, but nothing uncomfortable or dangerous. The sun was high in a clear sky, and there was an increasing chill in the air.

Kulikowski and Lyons were horsing around and having fun with Augulis. They had had plenty for lunch and more than enough beer. The fish had stopped biting. They needed something to do, after all, so they told Augulis that they were going to throw his sorry ass overboard. He pleaded with them not to play around like that. He yelled that he could not swim, and while there were life vests aboard, nobody was wearing one. Real men did not need such things. The two grabbed hold of Augulis, who screamed again that he could not swim and that they should not fool around like that with him. One got hold of his feet, the other grabbed him under the arms and they threw Mike Augulis, screaming and kicking, into the water. There was a big splash, some white, foaming water as he struggled and then total and complete calm on the surface where he disappeared from sight.

The three men in the other boat were astounded at what they had just witnessed, at the brazen coldness of the two men and at their utter stupidity. All five were numb with fright, but nothing equal to the fright, the fear, the utter terror on the face of Mike Augulis thrashing in the water in front of their eyes before he slipped below.

Quickly, they looked around to see if another boat was close enough to see what they had done. None was. Also, they were just a bit too far from the beach at Sandy Hook for anyone else to have seen them. It was still early in the boating and swimming season, June 5, 1999. With luck, they reasoned, nobody was watching with binoculars up in the Highlands or Atlantic Highlands hills. No one was. So the five made a plan; they took an oath to support one another with their silence. Lyons used his cellphone to call 911 to report the drowning of a friend from a boat on Sandy Hook Bay. Kulikowski slipped himself gently overboard into the water, getting himself thoroughly wet yet holding tight to the boat's gunnels. He took a quick glance underwater, saw nothing and figured that his dunking would suggest that he had made a valiant attempt to find poor Mike Augulis after he stumbled in the boat, clumsy as he was, sat on the side, accidentally fell overboard and sank beneath the surface before anybody could help. That was their plan. That was the story that each and every man told to the police and Coast Guardsmen when they came upon the scene of the tragedy, of the sad accident, of the awful loss and death of their friend and co-worker, Mike Augulis.

The rapid response of police and rescue departments was later noted and praised by Monmouth County prosecutor Louis Valentin. The U.S. Coast Guard from Sandy Hook was there with police rescue squads from six nearby towns, the New Jersey State Police Marine Bureau and even the New York City Police Harbor Unit. They were, of course, too late to save Mike Augulis, but they searched for his body for the rest of that day and part of the next with no result. The local watermen of Highlands knew that the river and bay would give Augulis back in their own time, in at least a week, sometimes in a few weeks. As Kulikowski's attorney years later would state, "The current was just too strong, and the water was just too murky." So everyone waited, most quite patiently, but the five men from the boats rather anxiously.

Not a week later, the waters returned Mike Augulis to the surface, on June 11, 1999. Fishermen out in a boat found the body and notified the authorities. The State Marine Unit was called, without hurry this time, and received the body. Based on a forensic examination and the reports taken the day of the incident, the death of Michael Augulis (age thirty-four, unmarried, standing five foot nine and weighing 160 pounds, with no permanent address and no known relatives) was ruled an accidental drowning. The file was labeled and put away. The case was closed.

Life went on for Kulikowski, Lyons and the other three men but, of course, not for Mike Augulis. Kulikowski and Lyons reminded the others that they were all in it together and had to stand strong and keep quiet "to keep the questions from coming." Their reminders were not all that subtle; in fact, the two big guys even threatened the other three to keep silent about what happened, according to the Prosecutor's Office. The trucking company in North Bergen, where they all had worked, folded and went out of business. Lyons moved away to St. Louis, Missouri, likely hoping that the distance from the crime scene would somehow isolate him from guilt. It did not. Kulikowski moved his family to a house in Sayreville, New Jersey, closer to the bay that knew his dark secrets, which, as deeply submerged as they were, would rise to the surface to meet the light of scrutiny in time.

Time went on. Years passed in total silence. The five had kept their oath to one another faithfully. Then, in late 2006, detectives with the Hudson County Prosecutor's Office were investigating some crime totally unrelated to the murder on the water seven years before. It is likely that they had one of the three men from the other boat in their interrogation room. He was being pressured about a crime he had done. The cops had him in their sights, and he was going to be charged with a serious offense, when he played a card he had kept close for many years. If they could make a deal, perhaps for a lighter charge or sentence, he had information about another crime, a murder that had taken place back in 1999. The details he supplied, the names he spelled out and the scenario he wrote down could only have come from an eyewitness on June 5, 1999, someone in the other boat.

Jersey City called Valentin in Freehold. The old Mike Augulis case file was pulled out and reviewed jointly by detectives from the Monmouth County Prosecutor's Office and the Major Crimes Unit of the New Jersey State Police. Simultaneously, on Thursday, November 30, 2006, investigators arrested Kevin Kulikowski at his home in Sayreville and Thomas Lyons at his place in St. Louis, Missouri. They were handcuffed and charged with the crime of aggravated manslaughter for the killing of Michael Augulis recklessly while manifesting extreme indifference to the value of human life. The newspaper accounts of the arrest noted that the offense was a first-degree crime and carried a possible sentence of thirty years imprisonment, which, according to the No Early Release Act, required that 85 percent of the sentence be served before parole consideration. Lyons waived an extradition hearing and was brought to Monmouth County in December 2006. Lyons and Kulikowski were brought before Judge Paul F. Chaiet, and they were released after each posted a bail of $300,000.

On April 2, 2008, a Monmouth County Grand Jury returned an indictment of first-degree aggravated manslaughter against Kulikowski and Lyons.

Monmouth County assistant prosecutor Michael J. Wojciechowski was in charge of the case. Christopher L. Patella of Bayonne, New Jersey, represented Kulikowski, and Thomas J. Cammaratta of Jersey City represented Lyons. The judge assigned to the case was Superior Court judge Anthony Mellaci, sitting in Freehold, Monmouth County.

The case, however, never went to trial due to a plea bargain agreement that had been negotiated. Kevin Kulikowski, thirty-seven, and Thomas Lyons, forty-three, agreed to plead guilty to second-degree manslaughter in exchange for the prosecutor's recommendation of a sentence of three years' incarceration, with the stipulation that 85 percent (or two years, six months and twenty days) be served before parole consideration. This was done with the consultation and agreement of members of the Augulis family, who had finally been located.

Standing significantly smaller in court than they had next to Mike Augulis in the past, Kulikowski and Lyons each individually pleaded guilty to the charge before Judge Mellaci on September 2, 2008. He set sentencing for January 9, 2009, just a few months before the tenth anniversary of the crime.

In that court session, Judge Mellaci stated, as he was about to impose the sentence, "This is a very depressing case. I truly believe you did not intend for this to happen the way it happened, but a life was lost here." He noted that neither man was an evil person but that the loss of life by their conduct mandated prison time. Kulikowski and Lyons were each sentenced to serve three years in a New Jersey state prison, with no early release before 85 percent was served.

Almost everybody was satisfied with the sentence imposed by the court. Judge Mellaci was satisfied. Assistant Prosecutor Wojciechowski was satisfied.

Prosecutor Valentin was satisfied. Defense lawyers Christopher L. Patella and Thomas J. Cammaratta were satisfied. Augulis family members were satisfied. Yet one person could not be asked if he was satisfied: Mike Augulis. He could not speak.

However, the editors of the *Asbury Park Press* spoke for Mike Augulis, as well as for all reasonable and responsible people, in an editorial on January 13, 2009.

> *Horseplay? Hardly. Two men who threatened to throw a man who they knew couldn't swim into choppy water and then did, resulting in his death weren't just horsing around. Their actions constituted vicious and willful mental torture. The three-year sentences they received Friday don't begin to serve justice.*
>
> *Before signing off on the plea agreements and sentencing of the two men, who faced up to thirty years for causing the death by drowning of Michael Augulis in 1999, the prosecutors and judge should have closed their eyes and imagined the absolute terror Augulis experienced in the last minutes of his life.*
>
> *As they held him in the air by his feet and torso in a boat two miles offshore during a fishing trip, Augulis pleaded with his tormentors, Kevin Kulikowski and Thomas Lyons, that he couldn't swim. They knew that. But they tossed him into Sandy Hook Bay anyway. Then they lied about it, and lied for years.*
>
> *Kulikowski and Lyons told investigators in 1999 that Augulis accidentally fell overboard. It wasn't until seven years later that another man who had been on the fishing trip, in trouble with the law on another matter, spilled the truth about what really happened. The prosecutors characterized it as horseplay that went too far. They're wrong. It was malicious torture.*
>
> *Threatening a man with an action he knows could take his life is bad enough, but Kulikowski and Lyons followed through with it, then quickly concocted a story to cover their misdeed. After their arrest in 2006, Monmouth County Prosecutor Luis Valentin said, "The evidence is clear that both the defendants knew the victim, who was their co-worker, could not swim."*
>
> *At the sentencing, Lyons told the court, "I live with the knowledge of what I did every day." Then why did it take seven years and someone else to reveal the truth about what had happened? The memories of Augulis' terrified screams should have echoed in their heads and made their lives unbearable. Instead, they went on with their lives, keeping their involvement in the horrific death a secret.*

At the indictment, Valentin said Kulikowski's and Lyons' actions showed an "extreme indifference to the victim's life." For that, and for their subsequent silence, confining them in a prison cell for three years isn't nearly enough.

Sources: Monmouth County Prosecutor's Office press releases, December 1, 2006; April 2, 2008; September 2, 2008; *Asbury Park Press*, editorial, January 13, 2009; articles on April 3, 2008; September 2, 2008; and June 9, 2009; *Star-Ledger of Newark*, January 9, 2009.

A NOT-SO-WICKED MURDER MYSTERY

With all of the murders, threats of murder and just plain talk and worry about murders throughout the Highlands, it was no wonder that Louis Boeckel went white with fright. His arms and legs shivered so badly that he couldn't keep rowing his boat when he spotted a naked foot sticking up out of the water in Clay Pit Creek in Navesink.

Boeckel's teeth chattered and his mind went racing, but not so quickly as his dash to the shore to get some help and to tell somebody what he found. All sorts of wild thoughts zipped through his mind. Was it a murdered body dumped in

Clay Pit Creek, a tributary of the Shrewsbury River, with steamboats passing through the Oceanic Bridge bound from Red Bank. This scenic spot was named after early nineteenth-century deposits of clay for bricks and ceramics.

the creek? Could it have been a suicide, someone who leaped off the Red Bank steamboat as it passed? Would there be a reward from the police? Or from the next of kin happy to have gotten Uncle George or whomever back?

On shore, he yelled to Bill Barry and Billy Snyder about what he saw. One ran and got a long, heavy rope, and all three went back to the crime scene in Boeckel's boat. All of them hesitated after they tossed the rope around the foot, for they knew that with all of the big crabs they had in the creek, the rest of the body was not going to be a pretty sight. They encouraged one another and pulled together, bringing the body to shore.

What they had was a body all right, but there would be no reward from relatives or congratulations from police. It was not really a dead body, since it had never been alive. It was a mannequin, clothed to appear to be a man, a motion picture stunt prop that had gotten stuck there in the creek. The Vitagraph moving picture company had been recently on location filming a scene of an automobile running out of control on the Oceanic Bridge between Navesink and Rumson and crashing into the river when the bridge opened for a passing sailboat.

Then they remembered that there had been another movie dummy used by practical jokers as a victim of reckless racing automobilists at night. These demented jokers used to wait until an automobilist was driving his machine at a good clip along the road, and then they would throw the dummy into the road under the wheels of the automobile. The poor driver would think that he had run someone over or even killed a man.

Louis Boeckel and the two Bills never dreamed of doing such a terrible thing with their dummy, but they did wonder if Vitagraph would pay a reward to get its dummy back.

Source: *Red Bank Register*, May 5, 1915.

Only Playing, Girl Kills Boy with a Bullet in the Head

The exact circumstances of a tragic event that took place in Leonardville on Wednesday, May 19, 1902, will perhaps never be fully known, since there were only four witnesses, one of whom was the killer and one the dead victim. The others were two boys named Hallum, who were neighbors of the victim and his killer. While Albert Card lived about an hour after the shooting, he was unable to speak as he lay dying in his mother's arms.

What was known, however, was that Albert Card, age eleven, son of Andrew Card of Leonardville (actually Navesink) near Atlantic Highlands, was shot in the forehead by Hattie Schruby, a colored girl, age about fourteen, of the same area. She was the daughter of William Schruby, well-known and respected hack driver in Atlantic Highlands, who stated that the girl appeared to be more than eighteen years old.

It was reported that all four of these children lived close to one another and often played together. The children's last game played together resulted in a senseless and tragic death.

An inquest was held the day after the killing in Posten's mortuary rooms on First Avenue, Atlantic Highlands, headed by Coroner John W. Flock of Long Branch. The empanelled men of the jury were Lewis S. Sculthorpe, F.A. Little, S.S. Morris, Lewis Foster, George Mackey and Matthew Brown. The Schruby girl was represented by William J. Leonard, and the state was represented by Prosecutor John E. Foster, both of whom were from Atlantic Highlands.

The jury observed the dead body and then listened to testimony presented by the Hallum lads and the Schruby girl. Their accounts of how the shooting occurred differed significantly. The boys testified, under oath despite their ages, that the Schruby girl took out a pistol from her apron, showed it off and then just pointed the weapon at the victim and fired, dropping it to the floor. The Schruby girl, having been sworn, stated that she was only playing with the revolver, that it fell from her hands to the floor and that it discharged when it struck the floor, striking Albert Card in the forehead.

The coroner's jury rendered a verdict stating that Albert Card met death from a pistol in the hands of Hattie Schruby. The members did not express an opinion as to the intent of the killer. Interviewed later by members of the press, they stated off the record that they felt that the girl had fired at the boy without realizing what she was doing, apparently being not fully developed mentally for her age, and therefore murder was not suspected.

Hattie Schruby was immediately taken to the county jail in Freehold early the next day to await action of the grand jury. The following day, she was released on bail to the custody of her father, after $500 was posted by William Schruby, William J. Leonard, Thomas H. Leonard and Jacob Stout.

In early September, the grand jury under Judge Fort, sitting in Freehold, was charged to consider the killing of Card by Schruby some five months before. Fort instructed the jurors that if they found that the boy had been killed through negligence, it was involuntary manslaughter, otherwise they could hand up a finding of murder and allow the trial jury to make further determinations. They voted in favor of a charge of manslaughter.

At her indictment for manslaughter the week of November 17, 1902, Hattie Schruby pleaded not guilty, and trail was set for November 26. The trial did not last long, and the jury could not agree on a verdict. Under the threat of being retried on the same charges before a new jury and on the advice of her counsel, William J. Leonard, Hattie Schruby pleaded guilty to manslaughter before Judge Heisley on January 15, 1903. The judge sentenced her to serve 365 days in prison and then suspended the sentence.

One has to doubt whether justice was served in the handling of the killing of Albert Card by Hattie Schruby. Key and crucial evidence was not brought forth at the inquest or the trial. The coroner should have had a physician describe the angle the bullet made as it entered the forehead of the victim. If it was from a steep angle, then Schruby's testimony might have been supported; if the angle was slight or almost perpendicular to the standing victim, then the account of the Hallum boys should have convicted the girl of manslaughter, assuming malicious intent was lacking.

The story of Hattie Schruby picks up some four years after the killing and is related in a *Red Bank Register* article of December 26, 1906:

POSTPONED MARRIAGE CAUSED BY SUDDEN DISAPPEARANCE OF A TRUNK

Miss Hattie Schruby and J. Weston Stokes, a Leonardville couple were married this afternoon by Justice Edward W. Wise, of Red Bank.

Stokes used to board with William Schruby, the father of the bride, and he kept his clothes in Miss Schruby's trunk. Now Stokes owed Mr. Schruby some five weeks rent and his soon-to-be father-in-law spirited away the trunk on the intended day of the wedding.

The couple chose to delay the marriage since neither wanted to have to purchase new clothes for their wedding ceremony and were determined to find the trunk before proceeding. They searched but could not locate the all important trunk. Mr. Schruby was tight lipped. They called in the police and an officer recovered the trunk after a brief talk with Mr. Schruby and an even briefer search.

The wedding clothes were recovered and the marriage took place. It is not known whether the late rent money was ever paid Mr. Schruby by his son-in-law.

Incidentally, Andrew Card, the father of the dead boy, was involved in another crime, the murder of Annie Leonard, wife of Charles T. Leonard, by Louis Harriott, in December 1891. Card was called by the arresting officer to positively identify Harriott as the farmhand on the Leonard farm in today's northern section of Leonardo where Leonard Avenue meets the bay.

Sources: *Red Bank Register*, May 21, 1902; May 28, 1902; October 8, 1902; November 19, 1902; and January 21, 1903.

How Not to Hide a Dead Body

The body of Joseph Mazza, thirty-one years old, was found horribly disfigured at 10:30 p.m. on May 13, 1919, near Valley Drive, Atlantic Highlands. Police Chief John R. Snedeker was expected to make an arrest that day.

The Jersey Central Traction Company's trolley was approaching the Y at First Avenue and was heading toward the Stone Church station in the last run to the Highlands. William Vunck, the motorman, and Gus Ahearn, the conductor, had just a few passengers aboard and were moving along the dark tracks at a comfortable speed of about fifteen miles per hour. As Vunck came around a bend, he struck something. He figured that it was a dog and stopped the car, and then he and Ahearn ran back with a lantern to see what it was.

Both men were horrified. Blood and mashed bits of bone, flesh and clothing were covering the iron tracks and the wooden ties. They warned the ladies on board to stay there—there had been an awful accident. What had been a man now was a bloody pulp all mangled under the wheels of the trolley car. Motorman Vunck noted that the time was 10:30 p.m. and sent Ahearn to the Atlantic Highlands electric light powerhouse nearby in order to send someone for the police. It was quite evident that a doctor was not needed. There were a couple of homes still burning lights not far from the scene. The house nearest the scene was in total darkness.

Bill Vunck was thoroughly beside himself, sick with remorse and shock. He figured that he had run over a drunk or a hobo passed out on the tracks. He had heard the trolley company managers speak of such freak occurrences. He knew that it was not his fault. Still, he felt just terrible for it all. How was he going to tell his wife that he had just run over and killed a man? Despite it all, he had to collect himself, had still to finish the run down to the Highlands and then turn around to head back to the junction, where he could report what happened and, along with Ahearn, hop a car to Keyport and home. How was he ever going to pass that place on the track, that death spot?

Maybe he would ask for a reassignment to another run, perhaps to Red Bank from the junction in Belford.

Atlantic Highlands police chief John R. Snedeker arrived within half an hour with two men from Amzi Posten's funeral rooms on First Avenue, as well as Dr. John H. Van Mater. The body, or at least the remains of the body, was removed from the tracks to the best of their ability and taken to Posten's place, where an autopsy was conducted the next morning.

What the doctor discovered on his preliminary examination was something bound to please the poor motorman, and as soon as he finished up, he personally telephoned the trolley headquarters in Union Beach to report the good news. The man had not been killed in a trolley accident; he had actually been murdered. He found and probed two holes blasted into the man with a shotgun, one in the left front shoulder and the other behind the left ear. In each wound, he discovered the wadding from the shells, showing that they were fired from very close range. The shoulder wound, he noted, was fired from a position higher than ground level, based on the angle it made in the body. He assumed that the one to the head was fired while the man was lying on the ground, having fallen from the blast to the shoulder. He also reasoned that the body was placed on the tracks in the hopes of disguising the actual cause and scene of death. His internal examination revealed that the man had lost a huge amount of blood, both from the shooting and from the trolley running over him.

The victim's name was Giuseppe (or Joseph) Mazza, not Anthony as had been first reported in the local newspapers. He was thirty or thirty-one years of age and single. A native of southern Italy, he had come to the United States about ten years before his death. He apparently had no relatives in the area and actually lived as a boarder in the home of his murderer for some four years, it seems, without incident.

He had been an army soldier in Fort Dix but had been discharged after about one year. Before and after this, he was employed in the Central Railroad of New Jersey Elizabeth port freight yards as a general railroad laborer.

The funeral was conducted without a clergyman at Posten's, at county expense. His remains were buried in an unmarked section of Mount Olivet cemetery in Middletown, New Jersey.

Before Mazza had entered the army, like so many men likely to be sent into the war in Europe, he made a will, leaving all of his possessions to his mother and a sister in Italy.

At about the same time that Dr. Van Mater started his autopsy, Police Chief Snedeker was at the trolley scene, where the body had been found the night before. What was clearly seen both disgusted and gratified the chief.

He quickly noticed dark bloodstains on the trolley ties leading in a westerly direction from the point of impact. He followed them carefully until they stopped. He was on to something big. From here the bloodstains led across the grass and stones for about one hundred feet directly to a house: the home of Peter Petragleo.

Snedeker saw a woman outside washing clothes in a tub. He assumed that she was the woman of the house and identified himself as chief of police. He got no intelligible response, for the woman spoke no English. He looked around and found a large amount of dried blood on the ground by the house foundation and near the rear door. This blood had been covered over with perhaps ten square feet of new sod, freshly cut from an adjacent yard, in a feeble attempt to hide the massive amount of blood.

Acting quickly, he stopped the clearly nervous Italian woman from washing the clothes, assuming them to be evidence, and removed them from the water. He saw that they were men's clothes badly stained with blood. He ordered the policeman with him to preserve them as evidence. Chief Snedeker, like Dr. Van Mater, now realized that the dead man had not been killed by the trolley but rather had died on Petragleo's property and also that the body had been placed on the tracks in a feeble effort by the killer to disguise the murder.

He sent his assistant with the clothes back to town, where he contacted the county detectives operating out of Red Bank to determine when they would visit the crime scenes. Meanwhile, he drew his pistol and assured himself that it was in good condition, just in case. He did not know where the man of the house was or even what his name was. He prepared himself for any situation. A visit to the neighboring homes and the powerhouse provided him with the probable time of the killing. The residents and the plant workers informed the chief that they had heard two loud shots the night before. That was exactly at ten o'clock, according to the power plant men. They also knew the people at the house: they were Italians, Peter Petragleo and his wife. They had three children. Petragleo likely was not at home as he was a section gang foreman for Jersey Central Traction, the trolley company. Petragleo's house was located on Avenue C a very short distance from the trolley tracks.

Monmouth County detective John Smith and county physician Dr. Reginald S. Bennett arrived on the scene shortly after noon. They were brought up to speed on the crime and all of the evidence by Snedeker. Mrs. Petragleo was again outside, again washing men's clothes in the washtub, and again she was stopped and questioned through an interpreter, the

Italian shoemaker from town, a man named Faruolo. The clothes were her husband's, they were bloodstained and they were taken into evidence as well.

Detective Smith, the police chief and the doctor agreed that a search of the house was called for. Inside Petragleo's bedroom was found a double-barreled shotgun which clearly, from the smell, had been recently fired, and from both barrels. Mrs. Petragleo stated that she knew nothing about anything that had happened. Outside again, after the detective had one of his men remove all the sod, the doctor took a sample of the coagulated blood to later be tested to determine its blood type and if it was indeed human. They revealed a large spot covered with blood that had been diluted with about a bucket of water. It seemed that the murderer had first attempted to wash away the blood with the water and then, realizing the futility of that, cut and planted a small lawn of sod over the hard, bloody ground. It all appeared rather foolish, the sod sections still separated and just sitting above the hard, packed dirt of the rest of the yard.

One of Snedeker's men stated the obvious: "This fellow who did the murder must not be very smart, maybe even a bit dimwitted." Detective Smith replied that in his experience most criminals were not at all intelligent, which was something that made his work easier.

After calling the trolley office to find where Petragleo was working, Smith and Snedeker drove up to Keansburg, arrested Petragleo in front of his men on the section gang, put handcuffs on him and took him to the jail in Red Bank, where he remained until he was moved to the county jail in Freehold. He offered no resistance.

County coroner Albert W. Worden Jr. of Red Bank held his inquest in Atlantic Highlands Borough Hall, which was located above the fire station on Center Avenue near First Avenue. The date was Wednesday, May 21, 1919. The complete list of witnesses included Mrs. Peter Petragleo, wife of the murderer; George Mordog and James Ryan, who had heard the shots and noted the time; William Vunck, the motorman, and Gus Ahearn, the trolley conductor, both from Keyport; Police Chief John R. Snedeker of Atlantic Highlands; County Detective John Smith; county physician Reginald S. Bennett of Asbury Park; and Dr. John Van Mater of Atlantic Highlands, who performed the autopsy at Posten's place.

Everyone except Mrs. Petragleo gave testimony, the substance of which has been related already above. Because Mrs. Petragleo was unable to speak or understand English, Rocco A. Faruolo was asked to serve as interpreter. This man was well known in town, having run a popular shoeshine and repair business at 78 First Avenue. It was said that his business suddenly almost doubled in volume once word spread in town that he had played a role in the murder investigation.

The arrested killer's wife testified that her husband and Mazza, who had boarded at her house for a few years, left the place together at about 6:30 p.m. the evening of the murder, seemingly to her to be in good humor and friendly at the time. She said that she did not know where they went and that she knew better than to ask her husband where they were headed. She said that she had heard two loud shots during the night after she had been in bed; however, she remained in bed, did not get up to investigate and did not know the time of night.

She went on to tell how she saw blood the next morning in the rear yard, and when she asked her husband about it, he said sternly that it was nothing. She testified that she saw her husband dig the sod from an adjoining field and place it over the bloody spots. According to her, he claimed that he put the sod there for the chickens to pick over. At another point, she claimed that it was she who put it there to beautify the yard. Mrs. Petragleo also testified that the clothes she was washing belonged to her husband but that otherwise she knew nothing about them.

Photographs were taken of the rear yard, showing the bloodstained earth and the sod partially removed, as well as the trail of blood leading to the tracks where the body was struck by the trolley car and the place on the tracks where Mazza's body was mashed by the wheels. Professional photographer John Di Fiore of Red Bank, who took the photos, attended the inquest and displayed his evidence before the jury.

The empanelled coroner's jury was headed by foremen Dr. Alfred A. Umscheid; others were Herbert W. Posten, Harry S. Roberts, John A. Stewart, Abram Siegel and W. Harry Posten. They viewed the body at Posten's rooms, surveyed the two crime scenes and listened to the testimony of all of the witnesses. After a short recess for discussion, the jury reached its verdict: "Joseph, also known as Giuseppe, Mazza came to his death by murder on May 13, 1919 at about 10 o'clock in the evening on the premises of Peter Petragleo and afterward the body was placed on the track of the Jersey Central Traction Company. Death was the result of two shotgun wounds, one behind the left ear, and one in the left shoulder."

The reason why Peter Petragleo murdered his friend and housemate Joseph Mazza remained uncertain, even after Petragleo's trial and sentencing to prison. It was supposed that drink, especially cheap homemade Italian wine, might have led to an argument over something. Perhaps it was something that Mazza said to Mrs. Petragleo. Perhaps he had made an advance toward the woman that enraged the man to commit murder. He never spoke of the murder or divulged his motives during the many years he served in Trenton State prison. Years later, in late 1930, after having served twelve years, Petragleo was released. He returned home, and soon his behavior started to become eccentric and violent. He apparently went crazy one night in late January 1931 while at home. He smashed most of the windows in his house and had to be subdued by the Atlantic Highlands police and restrained in the First Aid Squad ambulance so that he could be committed on February 1, 1931, to the Insane Asylum in Trenton. There he eventually died.

Sources: *Red Bank Register*, May 21, 1919; May 29, 1919; and February 4, 1931; *Long Branch Daily Record*, May 14, 1919; and May 22, 1919.

GOOD NEWS ABOUT A FEMALE RECLUSE PRESUMED DEAD AND MURDERED

People in Atlantic Highlands were accustomed to not seeing Annie Gill in the shops on First Avenue in town. After all, she had become something of a recluse some five years before her husband had died. She was getting advanced in her years, people figuring that she must have been about sixty-five years old at least. She was just an old lady, a bit grumpy perhaps, but she had a right to keep to herself if she wanted. Nobody had seen the lady for several weeks, not since about the middle of January 1910. Some Atlantic Highlanders assumed that she must have been a rich widow, and such talk was commonly on the lips of gossips; it wasn't just wealth in property, although the old hotel in which she continued to lived in the thick woods of Hilton Park overlooking town would have fetched a tidy sum of dollars. The loose lips prattled, as if from sure knowledge, that up there she was hoarding treasures in jewelry, furniture, tapestries and gold certificates. What nobody knew was that she and her husband had come from New York City in August 1891 and bought two acres for $1,000 on which to build what she called a boardinghouse.

A young lad who had just been tramping through the woods without anything important to accomplish, an impressionable boy named Ellis Martin, started something of an alarm about town. On his way home to Hilton Dock, he passed the old lady's house and saw a man on the first floor who opened a window and stepped out onto the porch. Catching sight of the

Martin boy, the strange man lost no time getting to a wagon he had in the woods and driving off fast toward the Highlands.

Police Chief John Snedeker listened carefully to the boy's account, thanking him for his concern for town safety. Examination of the house showed that it had been ransacked from top to bottom. Not a room had been spared. Everywhere bureau drawers had been pulled open and their contents scattered about the floor. In Annie Gill's bedroom, there was every sign of a struggle. But there was no Annie Gill, not anywhere.

As he was on the phone with Monmouth County prosecutor and detective Edward Minugh, Snedeker expressed his working theories: one, that the old woman might have been kidnapped, and the other, that she might have been murdered (strangled, since there was no blood noticed) and her body buried or hidden in the thick woods nearby. Somebody phoned the New York papers, calling the case a murder mystery. Several reporters came down on the trains and even filed inaccurate stories of suspected homicide.

The next day, the detectives conducted their own search of the entire house, attic to cellar. Again no trace of the old lady was found. They searched in the woods. Perhaps she had wandered off, as old people were known to do occasionally, and succumbed to the severe cold and wet, snowy weather. Again Annie Gill was nowhere to be seen, alive or dead.

At Snedeker's insistence, Minugh reluctantly agreed to a third search of the old hotel and premises. Then the police chief's men started yelling for Minugh to come fast up to the second floor. The county detectives were clearly embarrassed. There she was, frozen stiff on a small balcony porch, with the door closed. She was dressed in her house clothes, and overtly she appeared to have no marks of violence on her body.

The corpse was taken by order of Coroner John Sickles of Navesink to undertaker Amzi M. Posten's rooms on First Avenue in town. Dr. Harry Hendrick and Dr. John Van Mater performed an autopsy: Annie Gill died not from a violent act of murder but from organic heart disease. Relatives living in Cincinnati, Ohio, were notified, came to Atlantic Highlands and had Posten handle the burial of Mrs. Annie Gill on a bitterly cold Monday afternoon at Bay View Cemetery. Reverend Frank Fletcher, pastor at Central Baptist Church, where Mrs. Gill had been baptized in July 1900, laid a wreath on the grave and said the prayers of burial. The family spent no more time in town than necessary, and as soon as they had cleared off, the house was visited by curiosity and souvenir seekers, who looted every moveable object from the old house on the hill where Annie Gill died a lonely death. Yet at least she had not been murdered.

Sources: *Red Bank Register*, August 19, 1891; March 7, 1900; March 2, 1910; and March 9, 1910.

SENSELESS SLAYING OF ANNIE LEONARD AND MINUTE-BY-MINUTE DETAILS OF A HANGING

"Louis has always been crazy since his infancy; he always was an idiot." Such was the estimate of the killer's own mother, contained in a letter read to the jury by the defense team when Louis Harriott was on trial for his life. In a second letter, his mother wrote that her son was forever incorrigible, that she could do nothing with him and that in desperation she had given him two hundred francs to go to America.

Harriott should have heeded the advice of his first attorney after his arrest: to keep his mouth shut. On the contrary, he confided his guilt first to Dr. Long, the Monmouth County physician, and then to a few of his fellow prisoners at the county jail, who were all called by the prosecution to testify and relate the confessions they had heard.

He had been hired, he said, as a farm laborer by Mr. Charles T. Leonard through a New York City agency for a pay of twelve dollars per month, including room and board, starting exactly two weeks before the murder of Mrs. Annie G. Leonard. On that fateful day, Friday, November 27, 1891, in the afternoon, Harriott was told by Mr. Leonard to remove the pig manure from the sty and spread it on a field using a horse-drawn wagon. Leonard left the farm to go over to the train station for a few hours, a distance of less than a mile. Mrs. Leonard had sent her three children to play at a friend's house. She herself relaxed and worked on her hobby in the parlor, finishing a crayon drawing of a water scene. It was about three o'clock, and Harriott knew that Mrs. Leonard would be alone in the house. He picked up a five-foot length of rope and an iron fish plate or rail joining bar two feet long and went into the house to confront Mrs. Leonard and demand his pay of less than six dollars. She refused to give him any money, telling him to wait and speak to her husband. At that, he knocked her down with his fist, and when she started screaming, he tied the rope around her throat to silence her. Using the rope, he dragged the woman into a storage room at the rear of the home and struck her in the head with the iron bar to kill her. Next he took five dollars and a few coins and started out for Keyport, about twelve miles away, to escape. He swore that he had not sexually assaulted Mrs. Leonard, although he bragged to fellow prisoners that he had indeed raped her.

Annie Grover, the future wife of Charles T. Leonard, was born in 1854, the daughter of Clark Grover, a successful Middletown farmer; she had five sisters and two brothers, being the fifth child in the family. She married Charles in 1876. Their first child, Alice, was born in 1877. Then came Bertie (also "Berta"), a daughter, in 1883 and Charles in 1887. At the time of Annie Leonard's murder, the three children were fourteen, eleven and four years old.

Annie Leonard was known for her devotion to her husband and children, her family and her church, the Atlantic Highlands Baptist Church located on the corner of Highland Avenue and Avenue D. She was noted for her physical and personal beauty and for her brightness, charm, cheerfulness and amiable disposition. In the church, she was the infant class teacher for Sunday school. She also served as a prominent member of the Women's Christian Temperance Union. An indication of the affection and respect Annie Leonard inspired was the fact that for her funeral on November 7, 1891, the church was overflowing with mourners, and many had to congregate at the doors and windows in order to hear and participate in the service. The last hymn sung before leaving for the burial at Bay View Cemetery was Annie Leonard's favorite, "Rock of Ages."

Louis Harriott had been born Louis Aubertin on September 8, 1872, in Montigny, a town in the French province of Lorraine. Apparently, he used his stepfather's name, Harriott. He spoke French natively but had learned enough English to function in America since his arrival about 1886. He had attended school in Montigny but was not successful due to his violent behavior toward his schoolmates and teachers; he was marginalized as "incorrigible." His mother, who had remarried, had given up on him except for giving him the two hundred francs (about forty dollars). Harriott found only menial work in France and in New York City, where he finally found employment through an agency on Charles T. Leonard's farm in Atlantic Highlands or the Leonardville section of Middletown Township. His daily wage of forty cents was about half of the average paid to farmworkers at the time.

Harriott was nearly six feet tall, well built and muscular. He had a dark complexion, black hair and dark gray eyes, which were said to "shift uneasily in his head," considered a sure sign of deviancy or insanity.

Thinking that Mrs. Leonard was dead, Harriott panicked but was calm enough to take money from the dining room table and clean clothes and shoes from where he slept in the barn. Setting out across the open fields, he was seen hurrying and recognized by some people. This was at about 3:15 p.m., and he reached Keansburg by 4:00 p.m. and the Keyport steamboat dock by 7:00 p.m., about the time his victim's dead body was found. He intended to escape on the night boat *Holmdel* to New York City. The night watchman told him that the night boat had ceased running but that he could sleep in the cabin of the *Minnie Cornell* until the morning. Harriott gave as his excuse that he had been working at the Port Monmouth fish factory, became ill and was returning to the city. He slept soundly until four o'clock Saturday morning, when Constable Joseph Johnson of Navesink arrested him. He was given a hearing in Keyport and brought to the county jail in Freehold to await grand jury action, trial, sentencing and hanging. It was certain that Louis Harriott was guilty of the murder of Annie Leonard.

The Leonard children arrived home a few minutes before their father came in at five o'clock in the afternoon. The children said that their mother was not home and that they were hungry for their supper. Mr. Leonard was not concerned, assuming that his wife had gone to visit a neighbor who was

Railroad fish plate was used to bolt together the ends of steel rails, allowing them to expand and contract as needed. Louis Harriott used it to smash in Annie Leonard's head. *Courtesy Pine Creek Railroad, Allaire State Park.*

ill, typical of her kind way; however, he was puzzled that Harriott had left the horse and wagon in the yard. Alice, age fourteen, prepared supper for her sister, brother and father. After they ate, Mr. Leonard went quickly to the sick neighbor's house. He became alarmed when he was told that she had never come there at all, and he ran back to the house. Neither his wife nor the farmhand Harriott had come in. Now in a panic, at 7:00 p.m. he and Alice searched every room of the house. Only the old storage room remained. There a terrible sight met their eyes: stretched out dead on the floor was their wife and mother. Her face was distorted from strangulation, with the rope still tight around her neck; the back of her head had an awful, deadly gash from the iron bar thrown down beside her.

Charles Leonard acted fast, despite the emotional trauma he was suffering. He left Alice with her sister and brother while he ran to a neighbor to inform them and appeal for help with the children. He ran fast, like never before, to the station, where he telegraphed New York, Red Bank, Highlands, Port Monmouth and Keyport with a report of the murder and the name and description of Louis Harriott, the murderer. From the first, it was clear that Harriott was guilty, without a doubt.

Coroner Amzi Posten—hardware man, embalmer and funeral director from Atlantic Highlands—summoned twelve local men to view the body on Saturday, November 28. The formal inquest was moved from Monday, the day of the funeral, to Friday, December 4. In the mean time, he ordered Dr. John H. Van Mater and Dr. Henry A. Hendrickson to perform an autopsy. They found that death had been caused by strangulation by the rope having been so tightly wound around Mrs. Leonard's throat so as to leave a quarter-inch-deep furrow in her flesh. The head wound, they reported, was not the immediate cause of death, although it likely would have proved fatal in a matter of hours.

The physicians found no evidence of sexual assault, although they did find evidence of attempted rape in that her clothes were disarranged and her drawers underneath were smeared with hog manure and loam left by Harriott.

Harriott remained in the Freehold jail until Monday, January 11, 1892, when he appeared before Judge Beasley and pleaded not guilty to the charge of murder of Mrs. Annie G. Leonard. He was assigned two defense lawyers, William H. Vreedenburgh and Aaron Johnson. The trial was set for Monday, February 8, 1892, before Judge Beasley, and Harriott was returned to jail, where his defense team questioned him via a French interpreter. He expressed no remorse and said callously that he did not care what would happen to him, but then broke down, especially upon hearing his boyhood French spoken again, and wept several times.

The case for the state was presented and argued by two expert attorneys, Monmouth County prosecutor Charles Henry Ivins and Henry M. Nevius, former Civil War officer, hired to assist in this important case. Nevius astounded the spectators packed in the courtroom like sardines in a can and the defense lawyers with his fast-paced delineation of Harriott's guilt for the murder and rape of Mrs. Leonard. It was to be an open-and-shut case with witness testimony of Harriott's confession to both crimes. Charles T. Leonard, the victim's husband, and her two girls Alice and Bertie testified with great emotional travail. The crayon painting to which Annie Leonard had last put her hand, mind and heart was shown by Mr. Leonard and elicited "ohs" and "ahs" from the spectators. An expert witness was called, George Cooper, who had made a map of the Leonard house and farm so that jurors could relate to events and places relevant to the case. Next came the coroner and autopsy doctors, giving the jury all of the gruesome details of the fatal injuries inflicted. Finally, the prosecution rested its case after the testimony of the county physician and four jail inmates detailing the confessions Harriott made, thus sealing the fate of the murderer.

The defense lawyers knew very well that theirs was a hopeless case due to overwhelming circumstantial evidence and to Harriott's own confessions. Nonetheless, attorneys Vreedenburgh and Johnson attempted to present an insanity defense for Louis Harriott. Their desired expert witness on insanity and diseases of the mind was unable to testify due to being ill with pneumonia. Judge Beasley would not even consider an adjournment to allow time for the doctor to improve his health. Almost in desperation, he read Harriott's mother's letter into evidence:

Montigny, Metz, Lorraine, Germany
February 4, 1892
Monsieur Aaron E. Johnston, Freehold

I answer the letter you had the kindness to send us. Louis has always been crazy since his infancy. *From four to sixteen and a half years old he never did anything but go to school, but notwithstanding the watchfulness of his chief teacher when* he was taken with excess of mad rage and frenzy, *he did wrong all the same. But I assure you* he is not responsible, as since he was a child he always was an idiot. His craziness always excited him to fury *or passion. I assure you, sir, that these facts are as I tell you, as exactly as if God was telling it. You said to me that the trial was to be on the eighth of February. It is more than sure that my letter will not come in time, as I received yours February 4th., sent January 21.* But, sir, I implore your pity for him and for us, as he did not see the wrong before he did it. *Just to tell you, he wrote us a letter of abuse and reproach, just as if we had been the worst parents in the world, but I pardon him because I know what he is, and he don't feel himself as unhappy as we are. I pray to you to study him and* you will see that he is really crazy.

I am with respect,
Yours very gratefully,
Mother of the Great Unfortunate

The ultimate attempt to show Harriott's insanity was putting Louis Harriott himself in the witness box, risking a withering, no-holds-barred offensive by the prosecution that could destroy Harriott and their case entirely. The murderer admitted his guilt, something that only an insane man would do in court. He revealed that he had struck her with his fist not once but four times to keep her quiet. He testified that he had choked her and wound the rope tightly around her neck. The judge interrupted for a clarification, asking him why he struck her with the iron bar. "I did it because she was not yet dead. And I didn't want her to tell on me." Finally, Harriott swore that he had not sexually assaulted Mrs. Annie Leonard.

Near the close of the trial, on February 12, 1892, after the state and defense attorneys gave their closing arguments, Judge Beasley charged the jury. He spoke very sternly and solemnly to the twelve men. He stated that he considered the insanity defense to be pure rubbish and that Harriott showed no lack of mental capacity, since he had clearly planned and prepared his assault, waiting until Mrs. Leonard was alone and coming into the house armed with a rope and an iron bar, and since he had conceived a rational plan for escape, even bringing along a change of clothing and burying his work clothes in the woods.

Judge Beasley directed the jurors that if they believed that Harriott had committed the murder with premeditation, or if he had intended to commit outrage (sexual assault) or robbery and the murder was to hide the crime, then a verdict of murder in the first degree must be brought in. The jury was in deliberation just nineteen minutes and found Louis Harriott guilty of murder in the first degree for causing the death of Mrs. Annie Grover

Leonard. The condemned man collapsed and cried. Mr. Charles T. Leonard, sitting between the prosecuting attorneys, closed his eyes, spoke something to himself and then rose and thanked the two attorneys.

The next day, Judge Beasley opened court at ten o'clock in the morning. Immediately the defense attorneys moved for a new trial because insufficient time had been given them to summon expert witnesses and because Harriott misunderstood some key questions and statements due to his reduced intelligence and difficulty understanding English. The judge again called the idea of insanity rubbish and enumerated actions and statements on the part of Harriott that proved him sane and knowledgeable.

The judge ordered Harriott to stand and face him as he spoke. He advised him to seek spiritual counseling to assist himself in coming to

Louis Harriott, shown here in the souvenir photo card that he signed, "Louis Aubertin [his real name], age 19 years, 7 months, 6 days, died April 13, 1892." Boys hawked the cards for the Scott photographic firm on the streets of Freehold on the day of his hanging. *Courtesy of Monmouth County Historical Association.*

grips with the cruel, brutal and altogether unnecessary crime that he had premeditated and committed. He suggested that he would provide him ample time in jail for this and that he should not have any foolish hope of any relief in this world. Then the judge spoke the last words Louis Harriott would ever hear from him: "Louis Harriott for the crime for which you stand convicted, you shall be taken to the jail of Monmouth County and there remain in custody until Wednesday, the 13th of April next, and from that place you shall be taken to the place of execution and there be hanged by the neck until you are dead, and may God have mercy on your soul."

Supreme Court judge Beasley could hardly have selected a less auspicious day for the hanging. Early the day before, the process for the execution was well underway. The judge and Sheriff Smock each selected twelve men to officially witness the hanging; seven were physicians, and two of these were chosen to monitor the execution medically and to certify when Harriott was dead. Two clergymen and three reporters were allowed to be present, one from the *Freehold Transcript* and two from the Associated Press and United Press. On the day of the hanging, Charles T. Leonard was granted permission by the sheriff to witness the hanging of the man who had strangled his wife to death. With his son Henry's assistance, James Van Hise, the state hangman, constructed and tested the gallows during the night and again just several minutes before the time for the execution, set for ten o'clock in the morning. The gallows consisted of two strong vertical wooden posts, braced with iron, with a crossbeam resting on each. A heavy weight was calculated by Van Hise in size to properly lift and suspend the murderer when released by a simple lever so as to fall into a bed of sand. The gallows was located in a corner inside the jail, rather than in the open jail courtyard, to discourage huge crowds from attempting to view the hanging.

In jail, ten guards had been designated members of the "death watch" over Harriott, keeping him closely monitored in a cell close to the place of execution. His disposition was relatively calm and somber his last full day alive; he ate three good-sized meals, the sheriff serving him whatever he desired. Late at night, Harriott was visited by Reverend Kivilitz of St. Rose Parish in Freehold, and guards reported that he prayed loudly and fervently in French.

The morning of the thirteenth, Harriott rose at his usual time and bathed. Then he dressed in clean underwear and a neat black suit with a black scarf tie.

At 10:00 a.m., Harriott was allowed to address all of the prisoners; he admonished them to mend their ways after release and expressed regret over his fate, wishing that he had acted otherwise but never expressing remorse for his murderous crime against a helpless woman. Harriott then shook hands with all of the prisoners and guards and said goodbye to all.

At 10:05 a.m., the twenty-four official witnesses were sworn in and took their seats.

At 10:17 a.m., Harriott was taken from his cell to the gallows.

At 10:18 a.m., Deputy Sheriff Houston Fields read the death warrant to him, and Harriott started to sob.

At 10:19 a.m., just before his arms were pinioned against his body, Harriott shouted, "I want to shake hands with my old boss." Everyone thought that he meant Mr. Leonard, but Sheriff Smock quickly intervened, shook his hand and said, "All right. Goodbye."

At 10:20 a.m., Harriott's nerve faltered, and he almost collapsed standing under the gallows; the two physicians supported him as his feet were strapped together and a black hood slipped over his head. Harriott then recited in French the Hail Mary, the Catholic prayer. As the noose was fastened around his neck, Harriott sobbed the words, "Priez pour nous, pauvres pécheurs, maintenant et à l'heure de notre mort." ("Pray for us sinners, now and at the hour of our death.")

At 10:21 a.m., before he could say "death Amen," the weight was tripped, and Harriott's body shot up in the air, his head almost hitting the crossbeam. The body settled into the rope, with little twitching of the feet and arms, causing observers to conclude that he had not suffered.

At 10:22 a.m., Van Hise lowered the body until it was six inches from the floor so that the doctors could monitor the pulse and heartbeat.

At 10:23 a.m., 10:24 a.m. and 10:25 a.m., the pulse was intermittent, at about 128 beats per minute. At 10:28 a.m., it was 88 beats per minute.

At 10:32 a.m. on April 13, 1892, Louis Harriott was declared dead, but the body was left hanging.

At 10:43 a.m., the body was taken down for an autopsy, which showed that Harriott's neck had not been broken. A deep incision was made from the base of the skull to the middle of the back, causing a great flow of blood that made some of the witnesses fainthearted. The incision was sewn up, and the body was put into a coffin. The undertaker transported it to an unidentified farm about two miles from Freehold, where it was buried in an unmarked grave.

Some of the witnesses and many in the crowd, when they heard that Harriott's neck had not been broken, expressed satisfaction that he had died of choking from the rope around his neck, from strangulation, just what he had done to poor Annie Leonard 138 days before.

Boys continued to hawk souvenir photographs of Harriott to the crowd. One was special and considered a real collectors' item: a photo of Harriott, personally autographed by him the night before his hanging. He had written, "Louis Aubertin [his real name], age 19 years, 7 months, 6 days, died April 13, 1892."

The *Freehold Transcript* ran advertisements in all of the county papers: "Best authentic portrait of the Murderer; his history; two letters from his mother; his last confession; his execution. History of Monmouth executions from Colonial times till now. Three cents by mail to any address, and for sale by S.S. Sagues."

Sheriff Robert Smock submitted a bill for $500 to cover the expenses for Harriott's hanging. The Freeholders reduced it to $400. They also paid him $42.45 for the *per diem* wages of special officers needed to keep the peace on the day of the hanging. The total cost of the trial was estimated at $2,500.

Charles T. Leonard had a magnificent obelisk of granite as a monument erected over Annie's grave, the first of its kind in the newly opened Bay View Cemetery. His two daughters, Alice (died 1918) and Berta (1956), and son, Charles (1971), were buried here, and in 1925 his own remains were interred beside Annie's. While Leonard had remarried in 1894, his second wife, Mary Thompson Leonard, appears to have been buried on the site without her name being inscribed in a space left blank on the monument. Their son, David Charles Leonard (1950), was buried with his wife in a separate plot.

The actual hangman's noose used for Harriott was kept and was actually put on display in a glass case in Long Branch's town hall in 1894.

Sources: *Red Bank Register*, December 12, 1891; January 6, 13, 1892; February 10, 17, 24, 1892; April 6, 13, 20, 1892; June 15, 1892; August 10, 1892; December 21, 1892; and August 1, 1894; *New York Times*, February 13, 1892.

MURDER FLOODS INTO HIGHLANDS HOMES ON RADIO WAVES

The section title makes this story sound worse than it actually turned out to be. People throughout the Highlands area were worried, and they had a right to be, since after all there had been more than two dozen gruesome crimes of murder and mayhem committed in the Highlands' homes, hotels and even on the streets. Most dreadful of all was even the very thought of a death, let alone a murder, in a once happy home.

Even in 1930, few homes were affluent enough to afford one of those modern devices, the telephone or the radio. For messages, most people relied on letters handwritten and sent through the U.S. mail. Really important matters were sent by telegram, a thing that the Highlands people lived in fear of receiving, for it invariably brought bad news. People got the news from magazines and the papers. They had the Newark and New York City papers coming on the trains and steamboats, and for local news, everyone loved their weekly *Red Bank Register* and the *Atlantic Highlands Journal* or the *Highlands Star*.

Tubes for either model ran for $30, making the radio a major purchase, costing six weeks' pay in 1930, when the average salary was $1,365 per year.

Many people in the Highlands were old enough to remember when the "inventor of radio," Guglielmo Marconi himself, came to the Twin Lights to set up his wireless station back in 1899. Those were the old days of radio when telegraph dots and dashes, just like at the Western Union Telegraph office, were heard coming mysteriously out of a box connected to a massive series of long wires hung almost in the sky itself. Now, since 1925 or so, people were entertained with symphonies, operas, dance bands and singers doing popular songs heard on gramophones. Weekly variety shows gained in popularity until in 1930 dramas came into homes; whole families gathered after dinner around their radios in the parlor to be thrilled by crime stories such as the *Sherlock Holmes Mysteries.*

Then, for six nights in succession, starting seven o'clock, Tuesday evening, November 23, 1930, NBC (the National Broadcasting Company) washed the homes of Highlands with radio waves originating from station WJZ in the Times Square New Amsterdam Theater. It was the "Trial of Vivienne Ware," a drama supposed to represent an actual broadcast murder trial, something that most people had only read about in the papers. The cast of the drama were not actors but rather real-life people of the law. U.S. Senator Robert F. Wagner was the presiding judge. The prosecuting attorney was former New York City prosecutor Ferdinand Pecora. Counsel for the defense was George Gordon Battle, the noted New York Stock Exchange lawyer. Miss Vivienne Ware, on trial for her life and facing the electric chair if convicted, was, however, played by stage and film actress Rosamond Pinchot Gaston, "the loveliest woman in America."

The story had originated in the novel of the same title written by Kenneth M. Ellis. It told of a lovely society heiress accused of killing her fiancé, a noted architect, who was actually loved by a jealous yet beautiful nightclub dancer.

The *American,* a popular newspaper, sponsored the riveting drama and published exciting reviews of the action in each morning's edition, thereby fantastically increasing the paper's circulation. It was the first of its kind in radio broadcasting and offered money prizes to people who wanted to "serve on the jury" and mail in why they voted Vivienne Ware guilty or innocent. The best guilty and not guilty verdicts were featured in the paper. Some rival papers criticized the show, perhaps out of jealousy, for its commercialism, enticing listeners and readers with financial rewards. Newspapers reporting on the novel radio program alluded to the fantastic popularity of radio with the American family and especially the program featuring two noted "colored" comedians, *The Amos 'n' Andy Show.*

The novel and radio show were quickly turned into a Fox motion picture with the identical title, released May 1932 and starring Joan Bennett and Donald Cook, with the drama heightened by two attempted murders of witnesses during the actual trial.

Sources: *Red Bank Register,* December 3, 1930; *New York Times,* December 8, 1930; and April 30, 1932.

CRAZY THREATS LEAD TO THE INSANE ASYLUM

Joe Stankiewicz, the blacksmith over at the Old Stone Church in Navesink, and his wife, Ella, tried to do their best for his poor brother, John. They made excuses for him and his odd behavior. Stankiewicz knew that John wouldn't hurt a flea on a dog's back, but he did scare children and even adults with his bizarre language, his angry outbursts and his threats. Never married and jobless at age forty-eight, John Stankiewicz had been a sad case indeed since the day several years before when he was in an elevator over in New York that malfunctioned and fell several stories. He hit and badly injured his head, both physically and mentally.

John had been living in Highlands with John Horn, who let him do chores about the place to sort of earn his keep. That arrangement changed the day after New Year's 1907, when Stankiewicz started hallucinating and demanding back the money that had been robbed from him. He threatened in a disturbingly calm tone of voice to kill Mrs. Horn unless she gave him the cash that she had stolen, his inheritance.

Horn had police officer John Snedeker of Atlantic Highlands arrest him and throw him in the lockup for safekeeping. They took him before justice Grover Williams in town, but he dismissed the charge of assault and threat to murder Mrs. Horn due to insufficient evidence. Horn deliberately provoked Stankiewicz before the judge, telling him that he would never collect the stolen money since it never existed except in his demented mind. Stankiewicz then started rambling incoherently and threatening violence if he was not taken care of.

The New Jersey State Lunatic Asylum at Trenton, later renamed with greater sensitivity to New Jersey State Hospital at Trenton and Trenton Psychiatric Hospital.

Justice Williams felt justified in holding Stankiewicz in the lockup again until he could be examined by physicians and a determination made of his mental state. Two ordinary doctors observed the man in jail, spoke with him and conferred together. Dr. Harry Hendrickson of Navesink and Dr. John Van Mater of Atlantic Highlands agreed and certified that John Stankiewicz was insane. When Officer Snedeker agreed to take the man to the "crazy house" in Trenton, Dr. Van Mater corrected him and suggested that he use the current professional term: the "New Jersey lunatic asylum at Trenton."

Clearly, a century ago, being politically correct was required.

Source: *Red Bank Register*, January 9, 1907.

A DEADLY DOMESTIC DISPUTE

Two couples were having an after-Easter get-together and dinner at Felix Engle's house in Highlands on Sunday, April 24, 1921. The group of friends and relatives seemed to be having a good time: Felix Engle, Mr. and Mrs. Elmer Baldwin and Dennis Gallagher and his wife, Viola Baldwin Gallagher, from Brooklyn. Earlier in the day, the weather had been as fine as the disposition of all the guests. There had been some slight undercurrents brewing between Dennis and Viola, but the others thought that they were not too serious and would soon pass once they were all enjoying a good Highlands fish dinner (with local steamed clams, of course) and a few more beers to make everybody a bit more mellow.

However, the Gallaghers started trading a few sharp comments, and this led to a really loud quarrel. The others were upset by the angry behavior, and so the Gallaghers left the dinner table and went into an adjacent bedroom. The voices grew louder and more bitter. Then there was a few seconds' lull, followed by two loud blasts from a gun.

As the shocked Engle and Baldwin rose to enter the crime scene room, Dennis Gallagher himself stumbled in, said that he'd been shot and, unbelievably, walked three blocks to the offices of Dr. John L. Opfermann at Bay Avenue and Miller Street. The doctor gave the badly wounded man first aid and then drove him to the Long Branch Hospital.

The next day, Gallagher died in the hospital, but before he did, he signed a dying declaration statement that Viola had shot and killed him. The Highlands police hauled the woman, her brother, sister-in-law and Engle before George Hardy, the town recorder. He held Viola in the lockup for the county detectives

The scene of a deadly domestic dispute in which the killer swore that she had not murdered her husband, setting Miss Viola Baldwin free but leaving Dennis Gallagher dead.

and had the three others post bail as material witnesses. Elmer Baldwin and his wife complained that they actually had seen nothing and had only heard the shots ring out, without seeing who did the shooting.

In November that year, Viola went on trial for the murder of Dennis Richard Gallagher before Judge Samuel F. Kalisch in Freehold. She even took the witness stand to testify during the defense portion of the proceedings. The defendant admitted that they had had an argument and testified that Gallagher had slapped her face hard in the other room. He had been drinking quite a lot, she added, and often lost control under the influence of alcohol. Then Gallagher drew a revolver, she told the hushed court, to kill her, but she grabbed his hand and turned the pistol away from herself. The gun went off, striking Gallagher in the abdomen. Despite the fact that two shots were heard by the witnesses, she testified, "I swear I didn't murder my husband." As it turned out, Viola, age twenty-four, did not murder her husband, for she never had a husband and had never been married to Dennis Gallagher, age forty-four. She had only lived with him for the past ten years since she was fourteen years old. The jury found Viola Baldwin not guilty.

Sources: *Red Bank Register*, April 27, 1921; and November 16, 1921.

A Dishwasher's Dirty Business

The animosity and nasty words had been going on for some time between the dishwasher, James Shelton, age forty-six, and Moses Harrison, forty-four, a general orderly at the Ocean View Nursing Home, located at 88 Portland Road, Highlands, actually overlooking the Atlantic Ocean. No one really knew how the altercations all had started. What was more important was that they had ended with murder on Friday, April 16, 1959.

Police Chief Howard Monahan was the first on the bloody murder scene there on the third floor of the old Victorian-era house. And there was lots of blood, remarkable since there was just a single wound in the body. Once the chief got the whole story, he had to shake his head in frustration—lying on the floor in a pool of his own blood was neither of the two men who had been in the argument. Rather, it was a Good Samaritan dead on the floor and waiting to be zipped into a body bag for the Monmouth County coroner's autopsy, a thirty-year-old man named Israel Hill, also an employee.

Chief Monahan's report, which he turned over to the county prosecutor's detectives, William Mustoe and Merritt Kent, noted that a physical altercation, a punching and shoving fight, had broken out between Shelton and Harrison. The two stopped when Israel Hill intervened, and Shelton left. He went down to the kitchen, where he washed the nursing home patients' dishes, picked up a razor-sharp boning knife and zipped back up the rear stairs. He lunged at Harrison but missed him, plunging the big knife into the body of Israel Hill, who had courageously tried to separate the two.

Local magistrate Irving B. Zeichner ordered that the killer be held in the county jail on a charge of murder, without bail to await action by the grand jury. He gave Moses Harrison a thirty-day sentence in jail for disorderly conduct. No one ordered anything special done for the noble Good Samaritan, Israel Hill.

Source: *Red Bank Register*, April 23, 1959.

Billy Null Murdered His Old Man

William L. Null Sr. was killed by a bullet fired by his son, William L. Null Jr., at his West Garfield Avenue, Atlantic Highlands residence on Monday morning, July 26, 1937.

All over the little (and usually quiet) town of Atlantic Highlands, up and down the First Avenue business district, in every shop, in the grand Victorian homes on the hill, in the colored section on South Avenue and in the Italian neighborhood off Center Avenue, people had been buzzing all week about the first regular murder ever in town since 1923, when Andy Richard's wife was murdered by his brother, George. Not since the days of national prohibition and rumrunning had there been such violence committed in their rather proper little borough. Copies of the *Journal* and the *Register* flew off the newsstands. Commuters to the city on the Sandy Hook boats said that even the *Times* carried an article about the murder. Not surprised at all, they knew that this was no common homicide—when a son shoots and kills his own father before the very eyes of his mother. What a horrible thing! Poor Mrs. Null; first her brother dies (earlier in the week), and then her son murders his father! When it rains, it pours. What's next?

Atlantic Highlands Journal
Thursday, July 29, 1937

GRAND JURY TO ACT PROMPTLY TO INDICT YOUTH WHO KILLED FATHER AS MOTHER LOOKED ON. GAS COMPANY EMPLOYEE IS SHOT FATALLY BY HIS IDLER SON. NO REPENTANCE SHOWN BY KILLER. TRAGEDY IS RESULT OF REBUKE BY PARENT FOR LAZINESS AND BAD COMPANY.

Prompt Grand Jury action is expected in the case of William Null, Jr., who killed his father following a quarrel Monday morning in front of their home on West Garfield Ave., Atlantic Highlands. He was indicted when chief of Police Sterling Sweeney and other witnesses in the case were summoned to appear today before the Grand Jury in Freehold. Funeral services for William L. Null, fifty year old victim of his son's temper, took place at three o'clock this afternoon from his late home with W. Harry Posten officiating. Members of the staff of the gas company by which Mr. Null had been employed for nineteen years as night engineer acted as his pall bearers. Burial was in Bay View Cemetery under the direction of A.M. Posten.

The murder took place twenty minutes after the quarrel and in the presence of the wife of the victim. It was the second tragedy for Mrs. Null within two days as on the preceding day her half-brother Harry Mount had been drowned while swimming in the river at Highlands. Young Null who is twenty-one-years-old frequently had quarreled with his father who chided him for keeping bad company and refusing to work. The older Null kept chickens on the place and confirmed that his son even refused to help care for the poultry but persisted in passing his time in sitting on the porch and smoking cigarettes. Following their clash Monday, the older Null went out into the yard to work around the chicken yard and Mrs. Null stayed on the porch watching him. Young Null had gone to his father's room where he took a .32-caliber German automatic pistol from a drawer and shot from the window of his own room at his father who was about ten feet away. The bullet struck the victim in the left ear and ranged slightly downward shattering the jaw bone and coming out on the other side. The stricken man fell through a wire fence with blood streaming from his mouth. He did not lose consciousness but struggled to a sitting posture before the Atlantic Highlands ambulance arrived with William Gerkens, Edmund Gelhaus, Walter Anderson and Edward F. Hartcorn of the First Aid squad. Dr. Saul Rosenthal also had been summoned and arrived at about the same time. They found the wounded man sitting on the curb some distance from the spot where he had been shot. Mr. Null apparently did not realize the gravity of his injury and objected to being taken to the hospital and talked freely of the shooting. He said his son had frequently threatened to "get" him but he had not believed that he would carry out his threat. He died about two hours later in Monmouth Memorial hospital.

In the meantime the younger Null had calmly laid the pistol down on the front porch steps and gone to the police station where he told Sgt. Frank Gerkins "I've just shot my old man." He seemed entirely unconcerned and made the announcement as calmly as if he had killed a mosquito. He immediately was placed under arrest. Chief of Police Sterling Sweeney arrived in a few minutes and the prosecutor's office in Freehold was notified. Charles Frankel, Assistant Prosecutor, Chief Charles Tate and detectives Harry Zuckerman, A.M. Sacco, and Merritt Kent responded at once. The murderer made no attempt to deny his crime. He sought merely to justify himself by telling Mr. Frankel that his father had cursed him and used bad language in front of his younger sister. He complained also that his father had scolded him for "running around with queers and janes."

Following is part of a signed statement given to police by William Null Jr.:

"Did your father strike you or beat you when he scolded you for keeping bad company and not finding work?" Assistant Prosecutor Frankel asked. "No he never struck me but he swore in front of my sister. And all of a sudden the thought came to me to shoot him. He left the breakfast table and went into the yard to work on his new chicken pen. He was out there about

twenty minutes when I suddenly remembered seeing a revolver in a bureau drawer. The thought of shooting him came to me and I went to his bedroom and took the revolver from the holster. My mother was standing on the rear porch talking to my father who was sawing pieces of lumber at the side of the house. I went into my bedroom and saw my father thru the screen. Taking the revolver, without a word, I fired. My mother screamed as my father reeled with blood spurting from his mouth. My brother who was in the rear yard came running. And I walked out the front door and laid the revolver on the porch. My father staggered out of the yard and along the street to the corner about 400 feet away where he collapsed. Someone in the garage at the corner placed him in a blanket and called the ambulance. After the ambulance had left I walked to police headquarters to give myself up."

The prisoner was arraigned before recorder William P. Irwin and held without bail for the grand jury on a charge of first-degree murder. Sergeant Gerkens signed the complaint. He was taken to Freehold the same afternoon and locked up in the county jail.

Under the direction of Mr. Frankel, Null was taken out of the police lockup and back to the house, where he readily reenacted his actions at the time of the shooting. He showed the official where he had taken the pistol from his father's bedroom and also how he had fired from the window of his own room.

Forethought on the part of Sergeant Frank Gerkens prevented what might have been a second tragedy through the reenactment of the killing. The sergeant had been delegated to act the part of the murdered man, and at the last minute, he insisted on personally inspecting the pistol before the scene was enacted. It developed that, like most automatics, the German arm was designed to retain one cartridge. The remaining cartridge was removed, and the sergeant congratulated himself on his narrow escape from becoming a real victim.

A postmortem examination was performed by Dr. Harvey W. Hartman, Monmouth County physician, at the Posten funeral home in Atlantic Highlands. It showed that the bullet had entered the victim's head through the left ear, traveled downward, struck the spinal cord at the base of the brain and fractured the right jaw before exiting.

Young Null was the oldest of three children, the others being Emmett, nineteen years old, and Eta, thirteen. He was born in Highlands, where his mother had formerly resided, and attended school but quit at the end of the seventh grade. He never had worked steadily. He served two years at Fort Hancock and was discharged from the army several months ago. Since then he had been without occupation.

Murders—Some Tragic, Some Comic, All Wicked

The murdered man, aged fifty, was a native of Ohio and at one time served an enlistment at Fort Hancock. While stationed at the fort, Null met his future wife in Highlands, the town nearest to the army post and where soldiers habitually came for shopping and recreation in one of its two dozen liquor establishments. After his years in service, he took work with the County Gas Company. Several years before, he and his wife were separated, but she returned to him later for the sake of the children and because, as a Catholic, she could not be divorced.

Null was well regarded as a conscientious worker, on the eleven-to-seven night shift as plant engineer or fireman, by his fellow workers; neighbors said that he was a hardworking and industrious man who was reserved and minded his own business. His major past time was home-oriented: raising chickens.

Harry Mount, half-brother of the tragically widowed Mrs. Null, had disappeared on Sunday while swimming in the Shrewsbury River off Miller Street, Highlands. The *Highlands Star* of July 29, 1937, carried the following report:

HIGHLANDS MAN DROWNS IN RIVER
Harry Mount, 34, Disappeared in Channel Sunday While Swimming.
Body Found Tuesday on Shore at Sandy Hook.

The body of Harry Mount of Highlands, who was drowned Sunday in the river here, was found Tuesday afternoon on the shore at Sandy Hook, almost directly opposite where he disappeared. Henry Parker of Highlands found the body and notified the Highlands police.

Mr. Mount, who was 34-years-old, went swimming Sunday afternoon near the Neimark beach. He was swimming in the channel when he sank suddenly and did not appear again...He had eaten a heavy meal before entering the water and it is believed that he was seized with cramps.

Mr. Mount was born at Highlands. His parents, Mr. and Mrs. Isaac Mount survive. He also leaves two children, Raymond and Harry Mount, Jr. His wife, Anna Weiler Mount, died in April. Mr. Mount was employed at the Neimark service station, Highlands. He was a half-brother of Mrs. William Null, Sr., whose husband was shot and killed Monday by his son.

When arraigned before Judge J. Edward Knight in Freehold on October 8, 1937, Null entered a plea of *non vult*. The judge reserved until October 22 whether he would accept the plea and pass sentence or set a date for a trial. The assistant prosecutor, Edward F. Juska, recommended acceptance of the plea.

The plea of *non vult*, meaning in Latin "he does not wish [to dispute the charges]," is the same as the fuller legal phrase *nolle contendere*, or "to not wish to contend" or argue the charges. In either case, the plea is treated in the court as identical to a guilty plea, avoids trial and allows immediate judicial sentencing.

William L. Null Jr. stood before Judge J. Edward Knight on Friday, October 22, 1937, and heard his sentence for patricide. He was to spend the rest of his natural life in state prison. Sheriff's officers immediately took him away to begin his life sentence. No brother, no sister and no mother was there to witness the event.

"The law laid heavy hands on the Null family this week." So wrote the reporter for the *Atlantic Highlands Journal*. On Friday, the woman's older son, William, was imprisoned for life for the murder of her husband and the criminal's father. On Tuesday morning, the murderer's younger brother, Emmett Null, age nineteen, stood before recorder William P. Irwin in Atlantic Highlands and was sentence to 364 days in the county jail on a charge of disorderly conduct.

His mother filed the charge against him after Emmett had appeared at her new residence on Memorial Parkway and demanded that she give him money. He threatened to kill her if she did not do so. Following the quarrel, Null disappeared. A check by Frank Gerkens, acting chief of police, revealed that Null had deserted from the Civilian Conservation Corps (CCC) camp in Freehold several days previously.

This, unfortunately, was not the end of the sordid criminal affair. Emmett Null, just as his brother had done, stood before Judge J. Edward Knight in Freehold on January 14, 1938, and was sentenced to an indeterminate term in Rahway Penitentiary because he had escaped from the county jail. He had been at liberty just a few hours before he was captured in Matawan.

Sources: *Atlantic Highlands Journal*, July 29, 1937; October 14, 1937; October 28, 1937; and January 20, 1939; *Highlands Star*, July 29, 1937; *Red Bank Register*, July 29, 1937.

THE PENULTIMATE MURDER IN HIGHLANDS: A TROUBLING MYSTERY

Mary Ludwig was shot to death in her sleep at 4:00 a.m. on July 16, 1965. That was certain. However, what was not known was who murdered her and why.

Mrs. Ludwig, sixty, of Kearney, New Jersey, had been a summer resident of the Highlands for a number of years. This summer, she was on a two-week vacation from her job as a custodian in Kearney's Lincoln School and was enjoying the many relaxing activities that made the bayside town popular with visitors for generations. With her were her daughter, Dolores, Dolores's husband, Edward Gunner, and their four children, all of Teaneck, New Jersey. They were all staying in the summer bungalow at 284 Bayside Drive with their friend Joseph Rodgers, of Belleville, related to the owners Mr. and Mrs. Charles Rodgers, also of Belleville.

Grandma Ludwig was sleeping with her twelve-year-old granddaughter, Marie, in the rear corner of the house. All Highlands was quiet at the time, long after the many bars had closed for the night. Most houses were dark, and if anyone was on the streets in town, it was likely a recreational fisherman or one of the hundred clammers on the way to greet the dawn. Highlands had a reputation as a safe town, a place where summer kids could ramble all day long without a mother's concern. That still, dark morning, however, was not safe for Mary Ludwig.

The family was awakened by a loud noise, a gunshot, and found little Marie Gunner hysterical, running around and screaming for her grandma in a total state of shock.

Rodgers ran to get the police on Bay Avenue in the center of town, a fair distance from the Water Witch section where the bungalow was located. Police Chief Howard Monahan took the statements of the adults, letting the kids, and especially, Marie alone. The front and back doors had been locked. The murder room had three windows, one on the side of the house and two looking out on a screened back porch. He found the screens intact and hooked, without a bullet hole or even a tear. He noted down all of this information, and if he had drawn any conclusions from it, he kept it all very quiet.

The body of Mrs. Ludwig was taken away so an autopsy could be performed by Monmouth County physician Dr. Malcolm Gilman. He extracted a deformed bullet from the brain and sent it to county and state authorities in the hopes of identifying the type of gun that fired it, later identified as a small-caliber rifle. He reported that the bullet had entered the left side of the victim's face and head, without specifying the angle of trajectory the bullet took from the gun.

Immediately, Chief Monahan had a search conducted of the woods and brush in the entire area to possibly find the gun, if it had been thrown away by the perpetrator. Nothing was found, and the police knew that it would have been easy to throw it into the nearby river, where it might never be found. He noted that the hook on the screen door of the rear porch could easily have been picked open. However, he did not comment, except to county detectives when they arrived, that the shooter could have rehooked the door upon entering. But the shooter had to have exited in a hurry and would not have paused to try to rehook the door from the outside. If the doors all were actually locked, as the adults maintained, then either they were mistaken or someone from inside the house had to have shot and murdered the sleeping woman. That idea was countered with the question of where the shooter then put the gun.

John M. Gawler, chief of Monmouth County detectives, assigned three investigators to work with the Highlands police. They interviewed all of the residents in the area, without result. After a week on the case, the investigation produced no suspect, no weapon and no motive for the murder. However, Chief Monahan traveled to Kearney, Teaneck and Belleville to interview relatives, friends and acquaintances of the victim. When pressed by reporters, Monahan declined to comment, saying only, "Nobody saw anything. It's a real puzzler."

To this day, the puzzle remains unsolved, and this penultimate murder in Highlands is a cold case mystery.

Sources: *Red Bank Register*, July 19–21, 26, 1965; and August 4, 1965.

THE LAST MURDER IN HIGHLANDS

Whenever one writes "the last murder in the Highlands," it is done with the hope that the word "last" does not simply mean "most recent" and that there will not be a repeat of deadly violence in the community in the future. However, when people in a town allow their sense of right and wrong to be corrupted by illegal drugs and alcohol, the word "last" unfortunately never means "final" but only "most recent."

David Mason, twenty-eight, of Highlands killed his so-called friend Larry Fecteau, a thirty-eight-year-old boat and dock carpenter, of Fourth Street, Highlands, at about 1:30 a.m. on August 29, 2006. An argument of a personal nature began on the telephone and led to Mason going to Fecteau's house, where he summoned him outside as the argument turned physically violent. Mason repeatedly struck Fecteau about the head with his fists until the man fell to the ground unconscious. Police were summoned by neighbors awakened by the row, but Mason fled the scene before they arrived. Mason made no attempt to get medical help for Fecteau or to see if he was even alive. At Riverview Medical Center, Larry Fecteau died of his injuries six days later.

Later, Mason admitted that his actions caused the death of Fecteau in a plea before Superior Court judge Anthony J. Mellaci, who sentenced him to ten years in prison with the condition that he had to serve a minimum of eight years and six months before being considered for parole. Mason had two prior convictions, for burglary in 1999 and aggravated assault in 2004.

Sources: *Asbury Park Press*, September 21, 2006; and January 6, 2007.

Part V

Atrocious Happenings in the Highlands

ASSAULT ON A PARKER GIRL IN PARKERTOWN

The town of Highlands used to have two names: the Highlands of Navesink (the hill section) and Parkertown (the lower section), so called due to the extraordinarily large number of people named Parker living there.

Gossips were buzzing and had the whole of Parkertown on edge over the first assault of this kind ever recorded in Highlands, by one of their own and inflicted on one of their own girls, not just on that type of loose outsider from the city who was always thought to come looking for trouble. This was Florence Parker, the daughter of George Parker, a carpenter, boat builder and waterman (i.e., clammer). She was just nineteen years old, a member in good standing of the Methodist church at Parkertown and had always had a good reputation. She was above medium height, was rather attractive in appearance and wore a mass of glossy black curls. "Oh, the poor girl, and such a good girl, too!" These same words or ones similar were on the lips of every resident in lower Highlands.

According to her affidavit, sworn by her on the day after the assault, which took place on April 3, 1886, Mr. Charles H. Davis—also a member of the church, a class leader, trustee and superintendent of the Sunday school—attacked and raped her that Saturday evening. She was out walking a little before dark when Davis accosted her, saying that he wanted to talk with her a little on church matters and about his child, who had died a few months ago. She walked with him westward until she found night coming on and noticed that they had gone outside the village. She turned to retrace her steps, and her first suspicion was then aroused by Davis asking her to sit down. She refused and turned to flee; he caught her and threw her down. She struggled and cried aloud, but he threatened her if she continued her outcries. She resisted until she became exhausted and unconscious. The next thing she knew, she was standing up beside him, and he was supporting her. Her clothes were torn, and she said that he would pay dearly for his conduct. She returned home, did not sleep at all that night and could not eat her meals on Sunday. Her parents noticed her unusual behavior and, thinking that she was ill, proposed to send for a doctor. Then the girl told the whole story, giving as her reason for remaining silent so long that she was embarrassed and ashamed to talk to her parents on the matter.

It appears, however, that she had told John Robertson, who used to keep company with her, on Sunday morning at eleven o'clock. At the same time, Davis was in Parkertown. Robertson saw him and confronted him to demand why he had committed such an infamous act. They screamed and yelled at each other, using some pretty strong language. Florence had told Robertson that Davis had threatened to shoot her if she told anyone of the assault.

Charles Davis, age thirty, worked as a carpenter, at times with the victim's father. His wife was a cousin of the girl he had outraged. He was married with children, and on the day of the rape, his wife had been in Sea Plain, now called Spring Lake, preparing a new home into which they were planning to move.

Constable Joseph Johnson went looking for Davis with an arrest warrant in hand; the rapist, however, had fled to parts unknown and was not arrested until well after two weeks had passed. People read this as a sure indicator of his guilt, saying that you would never expect such a criminal act from a fellow townsman, a relative, a high-up member of the church.

Davis was indicted by the grand jury, posted bail, hired himself a Red Bank lawyer and denied that he ever assaulted the Parker girl. Again people read this as the act of a guilty man, for what innocent man needed an expensive lawyer? It was a good thing that he had an attorney, for his trial went badly for him on Monday, May 31, 1886. He was found guilty based solely on the word of Miss Parker, who testified in court against him; no medical examination was performed, and of course, DNA evidence would not be used until a century later. Charles H. Davis was sentenced to serve four years.

Then, after about only a year and a half behind bars, Davis was released, along with ten other prisoners, and pardoned by Governor Leon Abbett. Unbelievably, Davis returned to live in Highlands until at least 1900.

Florence Parker and John Robertson went on to get married, have a son (who was a beloved Highlands mayor) and live fairly happily ever after.

Sources: *Red Bank Register*, April 7, 14, 28, 1886; May 26, 1886; November 30, 1887; July 31, 1895; and January 31, 1900.

SIX NORTH JERSEY GANGSTERS AND THEIR GUN GIRL NABBED BY HERO HIGHLANDS COP

On Saturday, July 25, 1953, Police Chief Howard Monahan, assisted by Special Officer Charles Kinney, nabbed a gang of young, dangerous and heavily armed criminals from north Jersey; they had been on the state and federal most wanted list for weeks. The arrest took place right on the little and out-of-the-way Miller Street beach. Monahan was alerted by a sharp-eyed clammer, Harold Baker, who spotted a loaded revolver among the clothes on the gang's beach blanket.

Monahan changed from his uniform into grubby fishing clothes, arming himself with his tackle box, fishing pole, concealed badge, handcuffs and

The beach at the foot of Miller Street, Highlands, where Chief Howard Monahan almost single-handedly apprehended the gang on New Jersey's most wanted list.

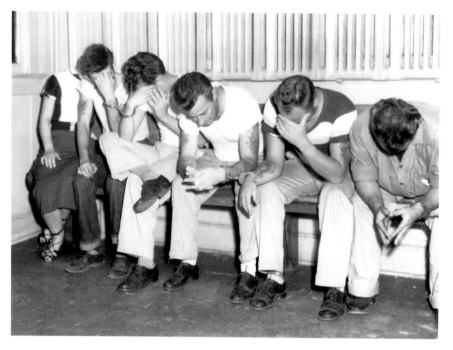

"Hoodlums" in Highlands Police Station sorely regretted their coming to spend the day at the beach in Highlands.

firearm. Pretending to be just a fisherman, he watched two members of the gang and their female companion. Then he moved in quickly, took them by surprise and arrested the three, confiscating a .32-caliber pistol. He brought them to the police station for questioning, where the three—Warren Davidson, twenty-five; Daniel Mahoney, twenty-seven; and Doris Kampmeier, twenty— confessed to break-ins and robberies in northern New Jersey. They told Monahan that four other gang members had rented a rowboat at Cornwell Street in order to dump a load of weapons into the deep water of the channel.

Monahan alerted the county detectives. They all waited for the boat to return to the dock, where they arrested Frank Rau, twenty-two; Leroy Davidson, seventeen; and James Kiernan, twenty-five. Ronald Cramer, twenty-seven, escaped but was quickly arrested on Bay Avenue. A search of Kiernan's car came up with two loaded .45s, three unloaded weapons and a quantity of gun parts. Also found was loot from several of the robberies committed by the gang in various north Jersey towns.

They told Monahan that they knew that the cops were on to them, after Leroy Davidson and Dominick Brionama, nineteen, had been

Chief Howard Monahan was a policeman dedicated to Highlands and good, honest police work for thirty-seven years. Recipient of the Valor Award of the New Jersey State Police, he was even more proud of the compliments from people in his town.

arrested in Elizabeth after breaking into the National Guard Armory there. Davidson had been released because he was a juvenile. It was he who then informed the others that the police would soon be after them. They resolved to dispose of most of the stolen weapons—thirty-six automatic pistols and six carbines had been stolen from the ROTC armory of St. Peter's College in Jersey City—in the Shrewsbury River and then to relax and enjoy the day on the beach in Highlands.

Little did they know that under Chief Howard Monahan Highlands was no longer the lawless clammer town and shantytown of bygone days. Monahan, other town leaders and lots of decent people were striving to make Highlands a good place to live, have fun and raise a family. The sun and salt water of Highlands quickly became for these hoodlums the dark and gloom of prison.

Sources: *Red Bank Register*, September 10, 1953; and October 22, 1953.

TAX COLLECTOR NAILED FOR STEALING BOROUGH MONEY

Scandal rocked Highlands on June 1, 1939, when longtime financier and businessman Grandin V. Johnson, age sixty-two, confessed to the Monmouth County prosecutor in Freehold to having embezzled more than $11,500 (his estimate at the time, which state auditors raised to close to $19,000) from borough tax accounts.

As the brother of the ex-sheriff of Monmouth County, Mayor Harry N. Johnson and policeman Howard Johnson, who signed his arrest warrant, he

Grandin V. Johnson, tightfisted in money matters, established a drugstore in Highlands in 1906. Here he expanded his business contacts, established Highlands' first lending library and installed the town's first public telephone, all designed to attract customers and make lots of money.

sought to avoid notoriety, trouble and embarrassment for them. He pleaded guilty before the judge in exchange for immediate sentencing to the Trenton State Prison for three to five years.

Grandin V. Johnson was proprietor of two drug shops, president of the Sea Bright National Bank, director of the Merchants Trust Company of Red Bank and president of the Highlands and Sea Bright Building and Loan Associations. He had been tax collector since 1907 and served as custodian of board of education funds and the borough water funds, being bonded for $15,000.

In about 1935, the borough auditor, John P. Mulvihil, reported to Mayor George W. Hardy and the council that there were irregularities—Johnson was caught using public money for private banking deals. No action was taken against him, despite the protests of the mayor, and Mulvihil was replaced by Charles H. Lomas, also the Atlantic Highlands auditor. Secret complaints to the New Jersey commissioner of municipal governments (likely by Mayor Hardy) led to a state audit already in progress when Johnson confessed. Lomas also confessed to embezzlement of Atlantic Highlands water funds and was taken to Trenton State Prison, having been sentenced to two to

A Borough of Highlands tax bill showing Johnson's signature as collector, an elected position he held for thirty-two years due to his efficiency and apparent honesty. *Courtesy Monmouth County Archives.*

three years, on the same day as Grandin Johnson, suggesting that the two had been in conspiracy to defalcate the Borough of Highlands. With Johnson gone, the new collector, John P. Adair, the former postmaster and reputed to be more honest than a saint, found many property accounts showing that no tax had been paid, some for as long as ten years. These properties were put up for tax lien sale unless the owner could prove with a receipt that taxes indeed had been paid.

Source: *Red Bank Register,* June 1, 1939.

Part VI

Crime Organized Right from Home

THE BOSS OF ALL BOSSES AND HIS DIRTY, DEADLY DEALINGS IN ATLANTIC HIGHLANDS

In Atlantic Highlands, people spoke with discretion about the mobster living right there in their midst, either out of fear of him and his associates or simply due to a habit of minding their own business—that is, if they spoke of him at all. Don Vito, as he liked to be known, was often seen on First Avenue in or around the shops, although he had necessary purchases delivered to his house or picked up from a shop or market by the several men known to be close to him. However, he did get out to enjoy a round of golf at times at the Old Orchard Country Club in West Long Branch or get a haircut and shave from a popular barber in Red Bank, where he occasionally frequented a couple of lounges on Monmouth Street. Otherwise, Vito Genovese kept out of the public view and even had his associates pick up and drive the barber from Red Bank to his home in Atlantic Highlands. Such behavior was wise for the boss of an organized crime family and especially for the boss of all bosses, as he ultimately became.

Genovese's Atlantic Highlands days came toward the end of his criminal career. It actually began shortly after the family's arrival in 1912 in New York, where the three boys Michael, Carmine and Vito spurned the usual Italian immigrant hard work and life in favor of a fast fortune coming from a life of crime. Genovese was arrested two years later for carrying a gun and served sixty days in jail. He soon found work with "Joe the Boss" Masseria dealing

Vito Genovese, in an undated official photo, here looking the part of a gentle and kindly grandfather, totally unlike the image of him painted in Maas's *Valachi Papers*.

in bootlegging and extortion due to his willingness to enforce business affairs with the blast from a gun. Genovese's killing of Gaetano Reina started the so-called Castellammarese War. Now associated with "Lucky" Luciano, who set up the betrayal and killing of Masseria in April 1931, Genovese was one of the four murderers. Next Luciano ordered the killing of Salvatore Maranzano;

Joseph "Joe the Boss" Masseria lived from 1881 to 1903 in Sicily, to which he had fled to avoid a murder indictment. In New York, he became an "enforcer" until he himself was "enforced" on April 15, 1931.

Genovese obliged, making Luciano the boss of his own crime family, with Vito Genovese as the underboss.

Also during the early 1930s, Genovese became very wealthy, bringing in huge amounts of cash, which he secured in safety-deposit boxes, due to his control of the numbers racket and the so-called Italian lottery. He used some of the money to buy into a few nightclubs in Greenwich Village, said to cater to homosexual clients. It was in one of these that he met and was thunderstruck by love for a woman named Anna Petillo Vernotico, a club hostess. Unfortunately, she was already married, and Italian social custom required a legitimate marriage and one done in church. Genovese was married, but his wife, twenty-eight-year-old Donata, died on September 17, 1931, in Brooklyn, leaving Genovese grieving for the usual six months. Anna's husband, Girad Vernotico, next was found strangled to death on the roof of 124 Thompson Street, Manhattan. His friend, Antonio Lonzo, who also was lured to the roof, likewise was murdered. This happened on March 16, 1932. On March 22, 1932, Anna Vernotico and Vito Genovese were happily married in a church in Greenwich Village. She was a loving and dutiful spouse, as well as a helper in her husband's business, but only for about twenty years, after which the marriage spoiled.

Next, things rapidly fell to pieces. Luciano was convicted of pandering charges and sent to prison, leaving Genovese as acting boss. However, in 1937, he was indicted for the 1934 murder of Ferdinand "the Shadow" Boccia. To avoid conviction and prison, Vito Genovese, despite his alleged love of America and his having become a naturalized citizen in 1936, escaped with a suitcase of $750,000 to Nola, Italy, a place close to where he had been born in 1897. Before he left, however, he set Anna Genovese up with access to deposit boxes stuffed with cash and settled her, with protection by Steven Franse, in his first New Jersey home. This was the Red Hill Road estate in Middletown Township, now called Deep Cut Park in the Monmouth County Parks System. (The original house was destroyed by fire and replaced. Otherwise, the garden features, resembling a miniature Versailles but with an eight-foot-tall Mount Vesuvius made of stone, were completed by Dominic Caruso, the contractor from Atlantic Highlands.) In 1948, Caruso bought the property from Genovese and then immediately sold it to a woman named Gladys Cubbage.

In Italy, Genovese prospered criminally under the fascist regime, even becoming a close associate of Il Duce, Benito Mussolini. Genovese, despite the distance from America, still had a long reach and ordered the murder of Carlo Tesca, the editor of an antifascist paper in New York who criticized and annoyed Mussolini.

During World War II, once the Allies had taken Naples and Rome, Genovese seized the opportunity to become a liaison officer and interpreter

Vito Genovese's first home in Atlantic Highlands, at 130 Ocean Boulevard from 1946 to 1952, was opulent, isolated from scrutiny and secure behind a large stone wall. Today it still retains features reminiscent of Genovese's design and ownership.

for the occupying military government. At the same time, he continued the racketeering and black market ring that he had started under Mussolini. Army authorities broke the operation, arrested Genovese and discovered that he was wanted for the murder of Ferdinand Boccia. Shortly after Genovese's return to New York on June 11, 1946, the federal prosecutor's key witness, Peter LaTempa, was found poisoned to death while in a jail for protective custody, thus ensuring the acquittal of Vito Genovese. He did serve a few months in prison, though.

In August 1946, Vito Genovese abandoned the Red Hill house and bought a second house, his first home in Atlantic Highlands. It was located at 130 Ocean Boulevard. The house was securely situated along the cliff overlooking the Atlantic Highlands marina and was surrounded by massive stone walls. It was truly palatial, built in 1925 on about four thousand square feet. It exists today and in May 2011 was for sale for $1,750,000, assessed at slightly less with an annual tax liability of $35,000. All of the criminal acts and "business" endeavors of Vito Genovese were planned and ordered from this residence from August 1946 until 1953, when he shifted locations.

While Genovese was away in Italy, his status in the crime family naturally deteriorated. Once Luciano had been deported, Frank Costello rose to take control, leaving little or nothing for Genovese, the onetime underboss to "Lucky" Luciano. By 1951, Vito Genovese was having dreams of taking out Costello and becoming the boss of the family. It was at this time that the United States Senate Special Committee to Investigate Crime in Interstate Commerce (known as the Kefauver hearings) subpoenaed many mobsters to testify; all invoked the Fifth Amendment and refused to testify. However, Guarino "Willie" Moretti, who had made it big in gambling in Bergen County and Deal, New Jersey, was chatty, playing with the committee and for the cameras, cracking jokes but never admitting to anything criminal. His big mouth got him killed at lunch in Cliffside Park on October 4, 1951, when four hit men ordered by Vito Genovese and Albert Anastasia shot him.

Worse problems were about to almost overwhelm Genovese, far worse than any threat from a man in his crime family. Disaster was brewing within his very own family—from his wife, Anna, mother of his two children, Philip and Nancy. For some unknown reason, Anna Genovese, now estranged from Vito and living in New York, sued for financial support for her and her children. The case was heard in Freehold in December 1952. Genovese claimed that he could not afford support payments, since she had left him. He testified that he had modest means, earning just $107 per week from his management of the Newark-based Genovese Trading Company dealing in waste paper and rags. Mrs. Anna Genovese went crazy. She told the judge that Genovese was worth a minimum of $30 million. She explained that for years associates of her husband would arrive at their home with suitcases and boxes of cash, all of which she was in charge of counting, recording and hiding away in deposit boxes in dozens of banks in the United States and abroad. Anna had committed the unthinkable sin: the violation of *omertà*, the breaking of a sacred silence in a crime family. Nonetheless, Genovese did not resort to violence against her, to the astonishment of every man in all of the crime families in America. Likely, Anna Genovese had powerful, detailed evidence stored away with a confidant that would be brought to the U.S. Department of Justice should she be killed or die under strange circumstances.

However, the thoroughly embarrassed Genovese did retaliate against Steven Franse, whom he had appointed to work with and protect Anna while he was away in Italy. He blamed him for Anna's defection and arranged for his murder, accusing him of being an informer. It was done on June 18, 1953, in a Bronx restaurant by Joe Valachi's men, Paquale Pagano and Fiore Siano, working silently with a steel wire tightened around Franse's neck. They did not want to disturb the other diners in the restaurant or ruin their meals.

Genovese's second Atlantic Highlands home, less expensive and less ostentatious, was used to support his claim in a Freehold court of earning only $107 per week. He lived here from 1952 until his imprisonment in 1959.

Genovese had to maintain his poverty before the court and yet had to pay the judgment that was awarded to Anna. First he sold off the furnishings of the Ocean Boulevard home for some $5,000. Then he sold the house itself to Dominic Caruso to satisfy the rest of the $32,000 judgment.

Genovese continued to reside in Atlantic Highlands, in his second home there at 68 West Highlands Avenue, a very modest house of 1,190 square feet on a corner lot built in 1952 by Dominic Caruso. Don Vito proved that he was indeed a man of modest means, moving in August 1953.

Criminal activity from 1953 through 1959 continued to be carried out from this home as well, especially during the year 1957, when Genovese attempted to eliminate all rivals to his becoming Don Vito, the "Boss of All Bosses." First, on May 2, 1957, Vincent "the Chin" Gigante tried to wipe out Frank Costello with a shotgun blast right in the lobby of the man's apartment building in Manhattan. It was blundered, allowing Costello to escape with severe abrasions to the scalp and a very big headache. However, scared stiff, Costello put the word out that he was stepping aside in favor of Genovese and retaining only his gambling interests. Next, on October 25, 1957, in the Park Sheraton Hotel barbershop, Albert "the Mad Hatter" Anastasia was sitting in a chair with hot towels about his face, trusting his well-being to his associates standing by. The barber removed himself, and two masked gunmen blasted Anastasia and fled.

Albert "the Mad Hatter" Anastasia (1902–1957) died suddenly on October 25, 1957, in the Park Sheraton Hotel barbershop.

Vito Genovese now was boss of his own crime family and the most powerful boss above all others. He expected to exert his influence at a meeting, a sort of organized crime convention, scheduled for November 14, 1957, at the rural estate of Joseph "Joe the Barber" Barbera. At this Apalachin, New York meeting were dozens of leaders of all of the organized crime operations in America and abroad. Genovese's great expectations were dashed as quickly as Albert Anastasia's life had been rubbed out—by chance and by the good police work of a

New York state trooper, the place was soon surrounded by heavily armed state police, road blocks were set up and the house was raided. Some fled in cars and some even on foot across the fields; although fifty men escaped, sixty-three were arrested, one of whom was a frustrated, disillusioned and angry Vito Genovese.

Greater disappointment and more violent anger for Genovese was soon to come, causing him to leave Atlantic Highlands, never to return again until one day in 1969. Enemy powers conspired to remove Genovese by framing him on narcotics possession and smuggling charges. He was convicted on April 17, 1959, fined $20,000 and sentenced to fifteen years in the U.S. Penitentiary in Atlanta, Georgia.

From 1959 to 1969, in his new residence, Genovese continued to rule the family through others: his brother, Michael, who visited him in prison, Tommy Eboli, acting boss and Gerado Catena, acting underboss. Under this arrangement, Genovese took care of three more men.

Anthony "Little Augie Pisano" Carfano, who had slighted Genovese by supporting Frank Costello, was invited on September 25, 1959, by Anthony Strollo to Marino's restaurant for dinner. By chance, Carfano brought along a lady friend of the family named Janice Drake, former Miss New Jersey and wife of comedian Alan Drake. Before the pasta was served, Carfano got a phone call warning him of his intended murder. He and Mrs. Drake left quickly in Carfano's car. Hidden in the back was Strollo's shooter, who fired one bullet each into the back of the heads of Drake and Carfano. Vito Genovese read about the murder in the newspapers the next day.

Once Genovese was locked away in prison, Anthony Strollo abandoned him and pledged his loyalty to Carlo Gambino. This offense probably cost him his life. On April 8, 1962, Strollo disappeared from his home in Fort Lee, never again to be seen either alive or dead. Genovese likely ordered the disappearance on the suspicion that Strollo had been part of the plot to frame him on the narcotics charge. Again the newspaper told the story for Genovese.

Relations of Ernest "the Hawk" Rupolo and Genovese went all the way back to the Ferdinand "the Shadow" Boccia murder in 1934 that had caused Genovese to flee to Italy. Rupolo had served time in prison for the killing but was released about the time Genovese returned to America, and charges against him were dropped due to the death of key witness LaTempa. Genovese did not mark Rupolo for death right away. He let him live his life in daily terror that it would end with a gunshot at any time and in any place. Ultimately, after eighteen years of emotional torture, on August 27, 1964,

Rupolo's body was found on a Breezy Point beach in Jamaica Bay. He had been shot several times in the head, brain, neck and spine; in addition, he had been stabbed in the chest, lungs, heart and stomach. This was the last murder ordered by Vito Genovese.

Genovese changed residences again, moving into maximum security housing at the U.S. Penitentiary at Leavenworth, Kansas. Finally, as his health deteriorated, he moved to the U.S. Medical Center for Prisoners in Springfield, Missouri, his final change of residence. Here Vito Genovese died of heart failure on February 14, 1969, surrounded by medical staff, prison guards and his brother and two children.

At the viewing in Anderson's Funeral Home, Broad Street, Red Bank, there were more plainclothes police, FBI and press reporters than mourners.

The next day, Vito Genovese returned to Atlantic Highlands one more time, staying just long enough for the hearse to slowly drive by his home and for the nervous Reverend Michael Lease to celebrate a requiem Mass in St. Agnes Church, where it is said Genovese had regularly visited, situated just two blocks from his last real home in town.

Sources: *Red Bank Register*, August 22, 1946; February 26, 1948; December 11, 1952; February 5, 1953; April 16, 1953; August 20, 1953; and February 17–18, 1953; Genovese, Philip A. *The Grandfather Clause*. Bloomington, IN: Author House, 2007; Maas, Peter. *The Valachi Papers*. New York: Harper Collins, 2003; Newark, Tim. "Hunting Down Vito Genovese in WWII Italy." *Crime Magazine*, June 2007.

About the Author

John P. King is a retired teacher of Latin and French at Red Bank Regional High School. Since owning a historic home in Highlands and running it as a bed-and-breakfast with his wife, Helen, he has been researching and writing about all aspects of the rich history of Highlands, New Jersey. He is a member of the Highlands and Atlantic Highlands Historical Societies, having held offices in each group. Over the years, he has contributed a large number of "historical vignettes" to local newspapers and has written and edited several history books on Highlands. Recent works that especially delight him are his *Clam Chowder and Other Highlands Stories for Children* and *My Grandpa Adolph and Me*, a children's story about Atlantic Highlands. King recently finished a work that returned him to his educational roots in Greek and Latin, "Murder and Mayhem in the Ancient World," which is in search of a publisher. King may be contacted at ka2fka2f@yahoo.com.

also
{ AVAILABLE }

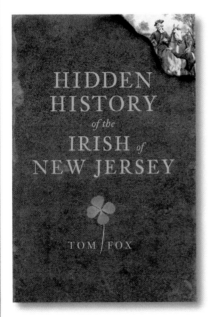

*D*he Irish have a long and proud history in America, and New Jersey is no exception. Beginning with the first Irish immigrants who settled in every corner of the state, this vital ethnic community has left an indelible mark on all facets of life in the Garden State. New Jersey's Irish natives expressed their own discontent over British oppression by battling alongside colonists in the American Revolution. Brave Fenians fought to preserve their new home in the Civil War. New Jersey's Irish also have become professional athletes, United States representatives, religious leaders, spies and business trailblazers. Author and Irish heritage researcher Tom Fox relays these and other stories that demonstrate the importance of Ireland to the development of New Jersey and the United States.

RETAIL PRICE: $18.99 ISBN: 978.1.60949.030.0 LENGTH: 128 Pages

IF YOU ARE INTERESTED IN HOSTING A BOOK DISCUSSION AND SIGNING FOR THE AUTHORS, CONTACT KATIE PARRY AT KATIE.PARRY@HISTORYPRESS.NET OR 866.457.5971, EXT 113.

We offer competitive discounts and monthly specials!
We are always available by phone or e-mail if you would like more information or to place an order.

We look forward to hearing from you!

MAGAN THOMAS
Sales Representative
magan.thomas@historypress.net
843.209.1255

MEREDITH RIDDICK
Sales Support
meredith.riddick@historypress.net
866.457.5971 x 121

also
{ AVAILABLE }

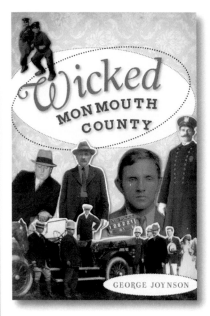

*D*uring the early twentieth century, Monmouth County saw more than its fair share of crime, conspiracy and corruption. In the midst of the Prohibition and Great Depression eras, Detectives Jacob Rue, William Mustoe ("the man who could make a horse talk") and Harry Crook investigated, and sometimes participated in, much illegal activity. The careers of these fascinating men included investigations of brutal murders, ruthless gangsters, an attempted cyanide poisoning, the kidnapping of the Lindbergh baby and a search for a vicious escaped leopard. From burglaries and bootleggers to speakeasies and swindlers, join historian George Joynson as he uncovers some of the county's seediest stories.

RETAIL PRICE: $19.99 ISBN: 978.1.59629.997.9 LENGTH: 160 Pages

Visit us at
www.historypress.net